The History of Sittingbourne Mill

by Richard Marsh and Steve Ralph

Published by
Sittingbourne Heritage Museum
2021
With the kind permission of Metsä Board

www.sittingbourne-museum.co.uk

The History of Sittingbourne Mill

SHM019
ISBN 978-1-911662-19-8

Published by Sittingbourne Heritage Museum, 2021
Registered charity number 1070698

Also published by Sittingbourne Heritage Museum:

The Story of Gore Court House and Estate, Tunstall
Family Businesses of Sittingbourne
More Family Businesses of Sittingbourne
The Inns, Taverns, and Public Houses of Sittingbourne and District
Sittingbourne High Street Volume 1
Sittingbourne High Street Volume 2
Historic Buildings and Grand Houses of Sittingbourne
A History of the Sittingbourne Co-operative Society
The Spicer Homes
A Look at Key Street's Past
The Rise and Fall of the Beat Groups in Sittingbourne
Wartime Heroes of Borden Grammar School Remembered
Sittingbourne in the Second World War
A Sittingbourne Miscellany
A Walk Through Sittingbourne in Days Gone By
The Story of the Convent of the Nativity School
East Street, Sittingbourne - A Historical Insight
Before the NHS: Sittingbourne's Health in the early 20th Century

Printed in the United Kingdom by Biddles Books Ltd, Kings Lynn

About the 2021 Publication:

This book was originally published by M-Real Sittingbourne Ltd in 2007, with proceeds from the sales going to Demelza House Children's Hospice.

The original was hard-back, and lavishly printed on many different grades of paper by Kent Art Printers. This reprint is a paperback version in different format and layout, but we have kept the original text and images, *so the information was current in 2007.* There have been just a few minor adjustments to text where the original might have led to confusion.

Sittingbourne Heritage Museum is a registered charity, and will split any proceeds from this 2021 reprint with Demelza House.

We thank Metsä Board and the authors for their permission to reproduce their fine work.

With thanks to Richard Marsh. Steve Ralph and Alan Amos.

Layout and publishing for Sittingbourne Heritage Museum by Allen Whitnell.

www.sittingbourne-museum.co.uk
charity no. 1070698

Changing Shift at Bowaters
Sketch by Nigel Wallace

The History of Sittingbourne Mill

Contents

Frank Lloyd – son of Edward Lloyd, the founder of the modern mill

This, then, is the story of Sittingbourne Mill based in a progressive town in which, over the years, many thousands of people have earned their living and contributed to developments which have had repercussions over such a wide area.

During the compilation of this book, M-real Sittingbourne has had valuable support from a number of sources. Firstly, thanks must go to all the employees of the Mill, both past and present, who have supported the project and made their own contributions. Included in these are long serving staff whose careers spanned many decades going back to the 1930's right up to more recent mill managers. Their contributions and memories can be found at the back of the book. Each one, in his or her own way, has worked hard to ensure the success of the mill over the years.

What has been noted by all the comments received is a common theme that Sittingbourne mill was like a second family to many people and that it is the friendliness and comradeship that will be missed the most.

Organisations including The East Kent Gazette, Sittingbourne Library, The British Association of Paper Historians, The Historical Research Group of Sittingbourne and Per Ågren of Media Bild have kindly allowed us to use text and illustrations in the book.

Thanks particularly go to Rexam for providing access to their extensive archive of photographs, books and other historical artifacts without which this publication would not have been possible.

And lastly, thanks to Kent Art Printers for their belief and support of the project and their enthusiasm to make sure that the book was published over a very narrow time frame.

Richard Marsh & Steve Ralph, 2007

Introduction – 2007

This book has been commissioned to mark the closure of Sittingbourne Mill after many years of paper making, and to provide a way of enabling valuable and cherished memories of the Mill and its employees and associates to live on into the future.

NICK CARTER - MILL MANAGER, M-REAL SITTINGBOURNE 31st January 2007

Records of paper manufacture on the Sittingbourne site date back to the 1750's, so it is not an easy task to truly reflect that amount of history in a relatively small book such as this, but it will hopefully provide a source of information to illustrate the key milestones witnessed by the Mill and its employees over more than 250 years. It is also serves to recognize the historical importance of the Mill to the surrounding area and to Sittingbourne itself.

There have been several owners of the mill during this period, most notably Edward Lloyd, Bowaters, Fletcher Challenge, and more recently, M-real. One thing common amongst all of them is that major changes have taken place in products, technology, equipment, working practices, and of course, people, and it is the people who have given their working lives and careers to the mill over many years to whom this book is dedicated.

I started work at Sittingbourne Mill as Engineering Manager in 1997 knowing that there were many challenges ahead. There was no doubt in my mind at the time that those challenges were possible to overcome. Indeed, a major transformation of the mill has taken place over recent years with the introduction of new products and new equipment, record production efficiencies, excellent safety and housekeeping standards, and consistent product quality for our customers. All of this has been achieved through the efforts, determination, loyalty and commitment of the workforce, management, and our owners.

However, the forces of global competition, increasing raw material and energy costs, and a shrinking market are the key factors which have led to the regrettable decision to cease paper making at Sittingbourne Mill. Clearly, none of us have any direct control over these factors, and it is no consolation that many other mills in the UK and abroad have also faced a similar fate. But this should at least help us to understand the reasons why the decision to close the mill has been made.

I would like to thank Jarmo Salonen (Executive Vice President, M-real Commercial Print Business Area) and Soili Hietanen (Senior Vice President, Production and Technology, M-real Commercial Print Business Area) for their support and approval to produce this book. In particular my thanks goes to all those involved in compiling the book including Steve Ralph, Richard Marsh and Kane Wootton of M-real Sittingbourne and New Thames Mills. A most sincere appreciation is due to all those past and present employees who have created the history of Sittingbourne Mill.

Finally many thanks to all those who have contributed photographs and information which make this book such a meaningful, memorable, and lasting record of the past.

N. Catt

The Early Years
1703 - 1863

So - when did it all begin? The earliest reference so far found is in the register of burials for St. Michael's Church in Sittingbourne when, on 14th April 1703, the burial took place of "Mr. Peter Archer, a Paper Man". The implication of this is that Archer had been making paper in the Sittingbourne area for some years prior to this. A later record describes another Peter Archer, presumably his son, as a "papermaker of Siddingbourne (sic)" when he married in 1708.

Peter Archer was still resident in Sittingbourne in 1720 and, presumably, still making paper. Another record shows that he had also been in possession of a mill in Chartham (south west of Canterbury) in 1733 so he was something of a papermaking entrepreneur in his day!

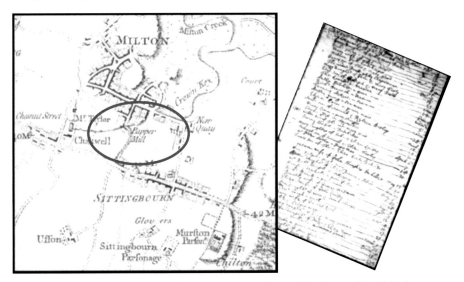

Copy of 1769 map. In the centre can be seen the site of the "Papper Mill", near to where the current mill is located. (Reproduced by kind permission of Sittingbourne Library)

Copy of register of burials for St.Michael's Church in Sittingbourne 1703

Archer was succeeded by William Stevens, probably a partner or former employee, sometime before 1749, at which time Stevens was declared bankrupt. The next confirmed reference is a map of 1769 which shows a paper mill on the site of the current mill.

On to 1786 and one Samuel Lay is described as a papermaker in an old book published that year. It is therefore possible that a member of the Lay family took over the mill when William Stevens became bankrupt.

What is recorded is that Samuel Lay, who already operated another mill at St. Mary Cray in Kent, took out an insurance policy on the Sittingbourne Mill for £2500 in 1785 and he continued to make paper at least until 1794 as witnessed by watermarked sheets found in a solicitor's office.

Sometime between then and 1820, the paper mill had been acquired by Edward Smith as there is evidence of hand made paper bearing the watermark "E. Smith 1820", again found in a solicitor's office.

By 1822, Edward Smith had become a man of affairs and a highly respected citizen as his appointment as Church Warden bears witness. He was not a man to be messed with as was later seen in the case of the sabotaged bridge! This started as a squabble between Smith and the man that built the bridge, blew into a legal storm and ended with Smith taking the law into his own hands.

Smith argued that the bridge obstructed the flow of water from his paper mill. Failing to get his way by law, Smith hired a gang of men who, in broad daylight, demolished the bridge. Today we may deprecate his action but it might also be argued that in breaking the law he also changed history. Without his action, papermaking may have died as an industry in Sittingbourne.

Although he continued to make paper at the old mill, his activities stopped abruptly shortly after 1850 but the exact date and reason for his retirement is not known.

What we do know from a report in the East Kent Gazette of 17th April 1858 is that the mill had been closed for several years and was rapidly going to decay. By the 1861 census, there was no evidence of papermaking in Sittingbourne.

Whatever the reasons for the decline of the mill during this period, the Archer, Lay and Smith families had laid the foundations for the future of papermaking in Sittingbourne.

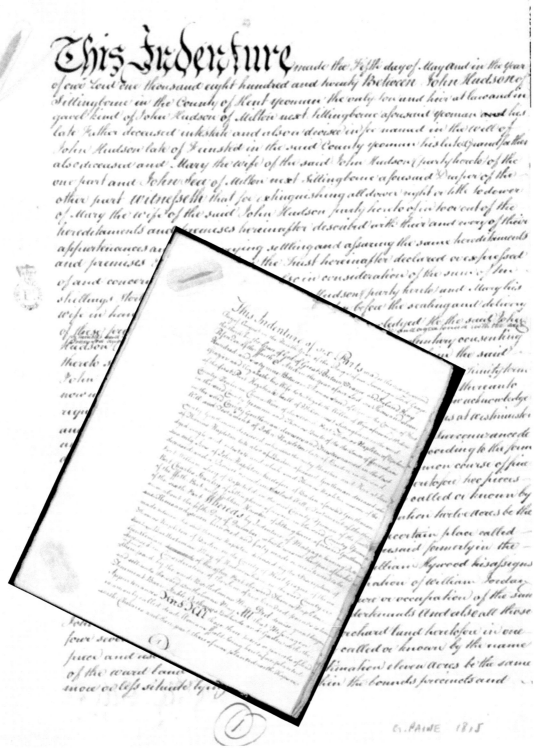

Samples of watermarked hand made paper from the Rexam Bowater archive. The smaller is an indenture written on paper carrying the Samuel Lay watermark of 1794. Behind is a similar indenture on Edward Smith's paper from 1820.

What sort of equipment would have been used during this early period?

Unfortunately, no details remain of the methods used in the process during these early years but we can make some assumptions on what would have been going on at the current Sittingbourne site then.

Full mechanisation of the papermaking process only started to be introduced in the early 19th century so everything before that would have been made by hand. The techniques used would not have been much different to the earliest method developed back in AD105 by Tsai Lun in China.

What is known is that a Frenchman, Nicholas Robert, was developing an automated system around 1798 and he brought the idea to England and sought financing from the Fourdrinier Brothers to continue his work. There is every chance that equipment based on his early designs would have been in use at Sittingbourne.

As Robert developed his principles, the level of automation increased as shown in the diagram below. It is possible that Smith had tried to move from making paper by hand to machine-made using Fourdriniers of this type. These machines were difficult to operate without skilled labour and this may account for the suspension of papermaking in 1858.

A diagram showing one of the earliest automatic Fourdrinier machines pioneered by Nicholas Robert in the early 1800s. This machine was 7.4m long, 1.5m wide and would have run at 7m/min and was originally installed at Frogmore in Hertfordshire. At the time of writing, one of these early machines is still preserved and in working order at the Paper Trail in Hertfordshire.

For a history of hand made paper visit
http://wildpaper.co.uk/html/
paper_history.html

The Lloyd Era
1863 - 1936

Edward Lloyd 1815 - 1890

The founder of the modern mill was Edward Lloyd, a young London publisher whose enterprise had quickly brought him from small miscellaneous publications to weekly magazines which were to be the forerunners of the country's Sunday newspapers. In order to obtain a good supply of paper for his own publications, he had already established a small paper mill in Bow, London. As his demands for paper increased, he acquired the site at Sittingbourne in 1863.

Initially, the site was used for storage and pulping of straw to supply the mill at Bow. But there is little doubt that, when he purchased Smith's mill, Edward Lloyd intended to establish a paper mill in Sittingbourne as he had no

opportunity to expand at Bow. It was not until 1876 that the first paper machine was installed on the site and records show that the mill was then producing 50 tons of paper a week on an old machine transferred from Bow. This was later added to in 1877 by the largest paper machine of its time - 123 inches wide (3.1 metres) and running at 200 ft/min (60 m/min).

Many a wise papermaker shook his head at this installation, for a machine of this width had never been heard of before. All sorts of trouble was predicted! But Edward Lloyd was again justified for the machine was not only trouble-free but, on the contrary, a great success.

The Lloyd Era was underway!!

The importance of this period to the development of the industry in the local area cannot be understated. Not only was Edward Lloyd a highly influential character in the newspaper world – he was owner of the Clerkenwell News and had founded the Daily Chronicle – but he recognized that there would be a requirement for the production of pulp from wood to replace the reliance on straw. He therefore bought exclusive rights to pulp from Honefos Pulp Mill in Norway.

In 1884, the mill was enlarged. A new boiler house with eight steel boilers was built, as was a 110 feet high chimney. By 1889 four machines were running in Sittingbourne, now known as the Daily Chronicle Mill, and the British and Colonial Printer and Stationer of July 11th 1889 carried a supplement showing a special engraving giving a view of each department (see page 20). Around this time, the census showed 140 people were employed at the mill.

Shortly before his death in 1890 Edward Lloyd was succeeded by his son Frank who, with his father's drive and enthusiasm, continued to develop the mill and by 1900 there were 10 paper machines in operation.

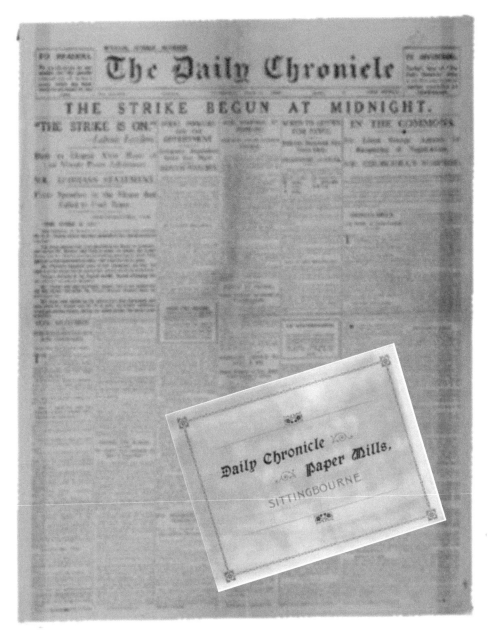

Daily Chronicle of May 4th 1926. By 1914, The Daily Chronicle newspaper, founded by Edward Lloyd owner of Sittingbourne Paper Mill, had increased its net sales to exceed the combined sales of The Times, Daily Telegraph, Morning Post, Evening Standard and Daily Graphic.

THE "DAILY CHRONICLE" PAPER MILLS, SITTINGBOURNE, KENT.

Reproduction of the engraving which appeared in British and Colonial Printer and Stationer of July 11th 1889 showing, in the centre, the four paper machines. Surrounding this are views of the other various departments in the mill, including the Beating Engines, the Grass and Rag Store and the Re-reeling Machines.

In 1890, Lloyds had became a Limited Liability Company with a capital of £250,000. By 1892, a new mill comprising a substantial complex of buildings was formally opened, with the architecture of the buildings being described as "in the Queen Anne style".

An early view of the new administration buildings of 1892. This is a rare view of the "pond" in front of the mill which was for many years a source of water used in the mill. By the early 1900's much of the pond had been filled in.

But the greatest expansion was yet to come. In the early 1900's, a further seven still wider and faster paper machines were installed. A contemporary 1902 article lists a total of 11 machines. Of these, seven were of British manufacture and the rest USA. Four were built by George & William Bertram, their widths being 103, 102, 115 and 125ins. Three were by Masson & Scott (118, 107 and 136ins); two by Pusey & Jones Company, Delaware, USA (90 & 94ins) and one by Bagley & Sewall (138ins). The eleventh – and newest – was No.11 built by Messrs. James Milne & Sons, Edinburgh.

For a feature on PM11, see page 24.

By 1912, Nos.15 and 16 machines had been installed. Both were 175 inches wide (4.4 metres) and capable of speeds of up to 650 feet per minute (200 m/min). The mill's production was now 2000 tons per week with a workforce of 1200. By the time Edward Lloyd Ltd was formed in 1910, Sittingbourne was the largest paper mill in the world.

In 1918, Frank Lloyd had disposed of his newspaper interests and devoted himself entirely to paper manufacture. By 1923 he had bought a large site at Kemsley which was to become the current New Thames Mill.

Nos. 9 & 10 machines, built by the Pusey & Jones Company, Wilmington, USA.

The Lloyd family had always regarded the social welfare of their employees as very important. The greatest testaments to this were the opening of the Clubhouse, the Sports Ground and Pavilion, the original swimming baths in St. Michaels Road and the Memorial Hospital by Frank Lloyd. His father before him had also been active in this respect.

There are at least two reports in the East Kent Gazette relating to Paper Mill employees Excursions. The first, from 1884, reports that "The workpeople employed at The Daily Chronicle Paper Mill … proceeded to Ramsgate by special train. The mill being shut for the day the party numbered close upon 400 men and women and a few boys. " Two years later and on Saturday 14th July "…. about half of the employees…. took their annual excursion – it being arranged for the remainder to go today (24th July). The party …. of about 300 left by special train…. their destination Folkstone. " On this occasion, the ".. excellent brass band of the mill…. enlivened the proceedings…. at the station yard.

Article from East Kent Gazette reporting the outing of 14th July 1886.

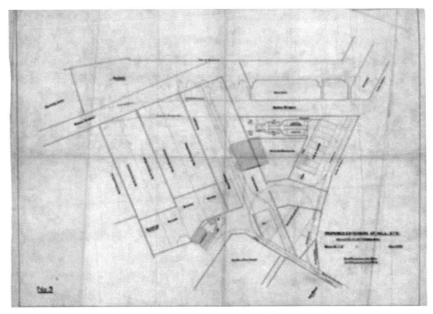

This plan of 13th July 1906 shows the proposed extension of the mill. The Old Mill Machine house is centre front and the extension shows where Nos. 12, 13, 14, and 15 machines would be sited to the left of centre. Top left is Mr. Denson's garden on the other side of Queen Street and right in the centre is an outline showing the location of the Manager's House. So we must assume that it was still in use at that time. Just five days later and a plan of 18th July no longer shows the house and Queen Street and the cottages on its north side are gone. No. 16 machine is in place alongside No.15, Queen Street has been moved north and part of the street has been re-named Jubilee Street.

As well as Frank Lloyd's elaborate plans for a housing estate on rolling land near to Kemsley Mill, a large Club House was built in Sittingbourne. The opening ceremony was on 9th December 1926 and this illustration is of the Commemorative Programme.

The Lloyd Era 1863 - 1936

A lengthy article in the November 1902 edition of The Paper-Maker and British Paper Trade Journal describes No.11 machine in great detail. Justifiably proud of his new acquisition, Edward Lloyd invited the (unidentified) journalist to tour the Sittingbourne site, as described here in the journalist's own words.

"The machine was manufactured, delivered, and started in the remarkably short period of five months. This is all the more creditable when it is remembered that the machine was designed from new – no old patterns being used. We really believe that this is a world record.

"The wire frame is very substantial and has many novel features, the side bars being electro-plated with copper to prevent rust. The couch rolls are of gunmetal, and the top press roll is of American hard rock maple. There are 24 drying cylinders, all 4ft. 6 ins. diameter, bored right through, buffed to a high polish and all felted. The framing is exceptionally heavy so as to avoid any vibration at the very high speeds. One of the novel features of the cylinders is the extra wide space between each so, as it were, to give breathing space – that is, to let the vapour easily escape. This must be a great boon to the machine attendant when leading through the paper.

"The paper passes from the drying cylinders to a stack of calendars of twelve rolls, provided with cold air blast. "Dillon's" doctors and self-feeds are fitted to all the rolls and are carried in side cheeks of a most massive character. The whole calendar has a very imposing appearance, standing some 16 ft. high from the soleplate.

"As can be seen from the illustrations, the machine is fitted with a very complete set of gangways back and front, hand-rails etc., so as to conform to the requirements of the Factory Act in every particular.

"In regard to the matter of high speeds, mentioned so frequently in connection with this new paper machine, we should say that speeds above the average are no new feature at Sittingbourne, where every possible inch is taken advantage of for the purposes of economy and increased output. Speeds of 350 ins. to as many as 450 ins. per minute are usual in these mills."

No.11 continued to run until 22nd April 1967. In its last week it produced 196 tons.

Transport during the Lloyd Era

When Edward Lloyd bought the mill, it was the perfect site as it had abundant water and excellent sea routes to major ports in the area. Several sailing barges were built by John & Stephen Taylor of Crown Quay and these were specially designed to move bulk cargoes of coal and straw in the soft bedded rivers and confined waters. Their flat bottomed, shallow draft allowed them to carry large, heavy loads in just a few feet of water and remain upright when the tide ebbed.

In the early days, barges such as this were used to transport raw materials and coal.

Premier – built by Kerr Stuart in 1904 and seen here restored in 1976.

But with 17 machines, this form of transport became a problem. Milton Creek was a narrow and twisting waterway and liable to silting-up. As the facilities along the Creek began to prove inadequate, a rail link was constructed from the old wharf at the head of Milton Creek to the Mill. Two steam locomotives – "Premier" and "Leader" – were commissioned in 1904 and 1906 respectively to bring coal and pulp from the wharf.

In time, this also became inadequate and in 1913 Lloyds began construction of a private dock at Ridham on the tidal Swale which could berth ocean-going vessels. The light railway was extended between Ridham and Sittingbourne Mill to enable wood pulp and raw materials to be brought direct from the dock to the mill.

Excelsior – built to the same specification as Premier and the third engine to be commissioned.

At its peak, the trains carried 200,000 tons each year but it is less well known that, by the 1960's, they were also providing a passenger service for Bowaters employees to travel in comfort from Ridham to the mill. It was a scheduled service, running 13 services throughout the day and night and it is estimated that about 75,000 people used the passenger trains per year. As road transport increased the railway became redundant and the official "last train" was on Saturday 4th October 1969. The railway is, at the time of writing, run as a tourist attraction as the Sittingbourne & Kemsley Light Railway (SKLR).

The official "last train" marked the end of the railway as a working operation.

The First World War Years

At the outbreak of war in 1914, some 716 staff joined the forces, recruiting being actively encouraged by Mr. Lloyd. Of these, 40 made the supreme sacrifice. Mr. Lloyd took a very keen interest in the men's welfare and every support was available to the families left at home. Nearly 650 women replaced the men, many coming from the families of the men.

The availability of woodpulp was severely restricted under the strain of war conditions and, with the need to keep the large newspapers of the metropolis supplied, the mill turned to the use of waste paper. Thousands of tonnes were sorted on specially designed tables and re-used.

Three paper machines worked to produce heavy brown wrapping paper for munitions purposes, producing over 200 tonnes per week. Throughout all this, the mill had some narrow escapes from air raids. Most notable was the memorable experience of the Zeppelin raid on June 4th 1915 when a piece of brass shell cut through the mill roof and struck a stoker a glancing blow on the arm!

The Mill saw some strange developments during the war, from drying soldiers' rain soaked sleeping blankets on top of the boilers to fruit pulping in No. 1 straw building.

The change from war conditions to peace saw the seven paper machines that were closed down at the start of the war back in production by July 1919. Likewise, the men returning from the war were swiftly absorbed back into the mill.

During the closure process in 2007, this example of an old smoothing iron came to light. It is the same as would have been used in a domestic environment in those days.

During the First World War, women played a major role in continuing the production of essential services whilst the men were away fighting. They were a recognised, fully trained workforce and took over all the tasks that their male counterparts had previously done. The girl in the left picture is using a hot iron to make a join using gutta percha as adhesive.

Special costumes and overalls were designed to provide comfort and safety amongst the machinery.

The Royal Visit

Soon after the war, in 1921, the mill was to host a visit from His Royal Highness the Duke of York, later King George VI. The visit is well reported in the July 22nd issue of The World's Paper Trade Review.

"On arrival, the Prince was received by Mr. Frank Lloyd, Chairman, to whose genius and organising ability must be attributed the remarkable development and extensive ramifications of the undertaking. The mill like the town of Sittingbourne and neighbourhood were gay with bunting.

"One of the most interesting functions performed by the Prince was an inspection of the Guard of Honour, composed of upwards of 300 ex-service men in the employ of the firm. The Guard of Honour represented men whose breasts were well covered with medals and its military bearing was most marked.

"The Prince, with Mr. Lloyd, the directors and visitors then made an inspection of the mill, which is typical of the most up-to-date papermaking methods in the world. The machine houses and the rest of the mill were noteworthy for their cleanliness.

"The Prince took farewell of Mr. Lloyd and left amidst the hearty and prolonged cheering of a large assembly to continue his good services in other directions connected to Sittingbourne. On the line of his route His Royal Highness had the opportunity of viewing the new sports ground which had been generously given by Mr. Lloyd for the benefit of the workforce."

One other function carried out by the Prince was to present awards for 50 years service to four employees – this was, remember, 1921!!

HRH The Duke of York, later King George VI, visited Sittingbourne Mill on July 14th 1921. This photograph shows HRH inspecting the Guard of Honour composed of 333 Ex-Servicemen from the Mill in the company of Major F C Gilham on the left and Frank Lloyd on the right.

The Tinder Box

Fire was a constant risk to the Lloyds mill, especially because of the huge stockpiles of straw and esparto grass used to make the pulp. No less than four fires were reported in the East Kent Gazette from 1863 to 1896.

In the report of 1863, the Gazette records that "stack after stack (of straw) had risen by degrees till their tops reached a great height..." The danger from this stack was well known by the locals and the Gazette reports that there had been concerns that "...a spark from the pipe of a passing smoker or the incautious use of lucifers by children to whom the straw offered a tempting playground" would result in a fire!! In the event, it was deemed that the cause was a spark from a nearby chimney.

Articles from the East Kent Gazette from 1863 to 1896 reporting various fires.

The Great Fire of 1900 showing damage to the Finishing House and Nos. 5, 6 & 7 machines.

By 1883, the Mill was in use again but a second more serious fire ravaged the area. The extent of the fire caused the Gazette to report that "... it really seemed as if the whole of the....buildings forming the mill ....in the construction of which wood had been largely used, was doomed" But "...the Milton Brigade worked their way into the interior of the mill....and played upon the fire with such excellent effect as to subdue it."

Another fire in 1889 destroyed an estimated 500 tons of straw and was reported by the Gazette as "One of the most destructive fires which have occurred in this district for some years…"

The fire of 1896 one Sunday morning was less damaging but the roofing of No. 5 machine was destroyed and there was much damage caused by falling debris. The Gazette reports that "The repair work was executed with such promptitude that the machine was running again on Friday."

Perhaps the most damaging fire occurred on 25th May 1900 when severe damage was done to the main machine house and machines 5,6 & 7.

Accidents were also commonplace in the Mill. Perhaps one of the most bizarre is reported in the Gazette of 16th November 1895.

It is reported that "….Harry Lindridge…. explained that Fosbraey (aged 14) had a piece of paper which he was throwing into the air, and trying to catch it in his mouth. Before the paper came down, deceased slipped, lost his balance, and fell (into the machine pit)"!!

Aftermath of the fire of January 1907.

The Changing Face of the Mill

During the Lloyd era, many changes took place at the mill, not least the architecture. This series of pictures shows the development of the Mill from the late 19th century onwards which included the construction of the fine administration building opened in 1892.

In the late 1800s, the machine house with four paper machines can be seen in the foreground. In the background is the creek with the Lloyds wharf on the left and the many sailing barges along the waterway to the upper right.

A few years later and this picture shows in the centre of the picture what was then the Waste Paper Department but which by 1892 had been replaced by the handsome administration building.

Early 1900s and the Administration Building is in place, alongside the "pond" from which water for the production process was taken. Compare this with the 19th century picture on p.12 – much of the "pond" has been filled in.

Some years later and part of the pond has been filled in. This picture also shows, in the foreground, the loop of the narrow gauge railway that transported raw materials from Ridham Dock. The shed to the left of the main building was used as a chlorination plant.

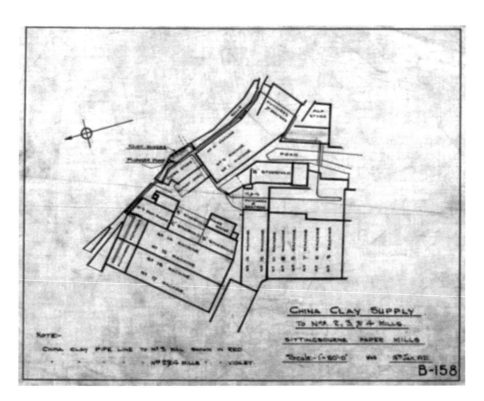

This plan of 15th January shows 15 paper machines in position (only Nos. 3 & 11 are missing). Nos. 1, 2 and 4 are in what was called "The Old Mill". The pond (centre right) is shown and this was eventually filled in and became the central road through the mill. By the closure in 2007, only two of these machines remained – nos. 15 and 16.

Those Dark Satanic Mills!!

It is difficult to imagine quite what it would have been like to work in the mill between 1900 and 1936 when the business was sold to Bowater. Some idea may be gleaned from this series of pictures which were last published in Bowlines April 1983.

It certainly would have been noisy - all the machinery was steam driven using overhead shafts and belts. Down in the boiler house, the stokers would shift anything up to 400 tons of coal every week to keep the massive furnaces running and the shafts and belts turning. All this coal had to be shipped in either on the barges or by rail and off loaded and stored at the mill.

Some indication of the motor power needed to run the mill was reported in the November 1902 article from The Paper Maker and British Paper Trade Journal. Here, the author describes the motor power as "...being supplied by two very fine compound Galloway engines, each of 400 HP supplied by eight boilers. In addition to the engines mentioned there were twenty smaller engines, with an aggregate 1250 HP driving various parts of the machinery.

"During the past summer (1901 ed.) a splendid main drive engine was put in by Messrs. Pollit & Wigzell. It is designed to drive 1600 HP when working with a steam pressure of from 100 to 120 lb. The flywheel is 20 ft. in

The boiler house. The hungry furnaces needed constant feeding to produce steam to dry the paper and drive the steam engines.

Pollit & Wigzell 1600 HP drive engine installed in 1901.

diameter, weighs 58 tons and is grooved for thirty six ropes. This engine was put down to replace one of 700 HP and another of 500 HP and is used to drive

the whole of the beaters on the New Mill side, supplying pulp for seven paper machines."

A safety officer's nightmare! This was the maintenance engineering workshop at the turn of the century. The man standing in the foreground has to be the Foreman because he is the only man wearing a jacket! Jackets like this were worn right up until the 1950's when white coats defined the Foreman's status.

It was not until the mid-1950's that overhead line shafts were disposed of in favour of individual motors for each machine to improve safety standards. Pollit & Wigzell 1600 HP drive engine installed in 1901. The boiler house. The hungry furnaces needed constant feeding to produce steam to dry the paper and drive the steam engines.

Likewise the various fibre products would be shipped up from the dock, either direct into the mill or into the massive sheds which later became a reel store area (Nichols Yard) and more recently a retail park. This was a serious fire risk and we have already seen (p.18) how many fires the mill suffered in the late 19th century.

Whether rags, straw or esparto, the fibre products were subjected to pulping and bleaching and the process is described in great detail in a 1920 publication, A Text-Book of Paper-Making by Cross & Bevan. The essential chemical for the pulping process would have been caustic soda (sodium hydroxide) with some lime being used depending on the source of the fibre. The fibre would have been boiled up for several hours in large pressurised vats of caustic soda. All the bleaching processes described in this book refer to the use of elemental chlorine. In today's modern Health & Safety conscious world, both of these chemicals would be considered very unhealthy for both the workforce and the environment so one can only speculate quite what it would have been like handling them in those days.

Rags collected from the London area would have been sorted depending on their quality – colour, strength and material – and hard substances such as buttons removed before being cut into pieces for treatment with caustic soda. Here this is all being done under the eagle eye of the matronly figure on the left. This photograph is actually of Springfield Mill, Maidstone and is thought to be about 1906. Reproduced with kind permission of the British Association of Paper Historians.

The beater floor in the Old Mill.

The bleached pulp – known at this stage as "halfstuff" – would then be transferred to the beater floors. Here, the pulp would be treated to "... separate the fibres into independent units each floating freely in the suspending liquid for realizing their felting and interlacing qualities in the formation of the paper." (Source – Cross & Bevan) It was not until the late 1940's that the now familiar refiners replaced beaters.

The beater floor in the New Mill. The man in the foreground looks as if he is stirring a vast Christmas pudding! But we think he is just keeping the pulp on the move! Note the "chef's" hats worn by the operators.

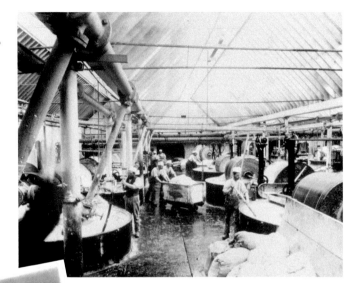

A postcard. Unfortunately undated, showing women sorting waste paper.

A view of the paper sheds at the wharf. Note the four legged mode of transport before it was replaced with motor power.

The Lloyd Era 1863 - 1936

There is no record of how many people would have been employed in these early years but it must have run into several hundred. Even in the 1940's, each paper machine would have had a crew of at least 6 – the most senior being the Machineman, then came the Dryer, Spare Dryer, First Boy, Second Boy and the Press Boy. Many other tradesmen worked for the mill including pattern makers, welders, blacksmiths, painters, carpenters, fitters, rope makers, foundry men and barge repairers. They even had their own fire engine and firemen.

A recollection from Don Rouse, a former employee who started work in 1936, tells of his elder brother who worked as dryerman in the 1930's. "In those days," says Don "the machine calender rolls had to be fed by hand – there were no rope feeds! The dryerman would sit on a plank with the calender rolls thundering in front of him and the last machine cylinder behind him. As the tail came through, he would grab it and throw it into the first nip. On one occasion, as my brother threw the tail, his feet came up and his toes went into the rolls!!! Did him a good turn as it excused him from army service!!"

Mr. T.E. Denson – Mill Manager in the 1890's - in his study in Brightside.

Many people spent their whole lives working in the mill and this was not unusual. As noted earlier (page 22) the work force were well looked after by the company. Houses were built in Milton and Kemsley for the workers; social clubhouses and sports facilities were provided around the local area and, in 1930, the Memorial Hospital was built in memory of Frank Lloyd.

That is not to say that working conditions in the mill were easy. It was not exactly pleasant for the local residents either. Even in the nineteenth century residents were complaining about the pollution from the chimneys which were showering the area with smoke, fine ash and sulphuric acid.

The mill used the excuse that it was having to use an inferior quality of coal! Other complaints concerned the foul smell coming from the creek during the hotter weather. But little was done and this was still a problem into the 1950's. Fortunately, this is no longer the case and fish can now be found right up to the upper reaches of the creek.

Possibly the most fortunate mill employee was the Mill Manager. Towards the rear of the site was his substantial residence called Brightside, sadly demolished to make way for more paper machines in the New Mill around 1907.

Brightside - the Mill Manager's residence.

The Lloyd Era 1863 - 1936

Reeling Room New Mill

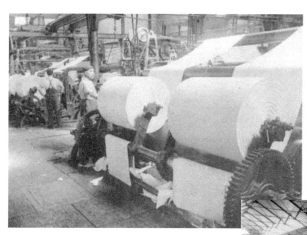

Nos. 5 & 6 machines

The pace hots up at the dry end of a machine. Notice the reels Nos. 5 & 6 machines being carefully moved under the watchful eye of a machine man.

The last Board Meeting minutes signed by Frank Lloyd – 23rd February 1927

When Frank Lloyd died in 1927, the control of the company was taken over by brothers Sir William and Sir Gomer Berry. The price paid by the Berrys for control was £3.2m and there is no doubt that they bought themselves a solidly prosperous business, built on an order book that was well filled with long running contracts. Profits for the years immediately before the takeover were certified as follows:

1923 - £310,407
1924 - £305,272
1925 - £390,073
1926 - £255,975

Then, one evening in 1936, Sir William Berry was dining with Ian Bowater, then Sales Director of the Bowater Group, who later recalls that Sir William turned to him and said "I can't think what you fellows are doing with that paper mill of yours. Why don't you buy ours? We are not professional newsprint manufacturers, we are journalists. We don't want a whacking great paper mill at Sittingbourne or Kemsley – that is your job."

The rest, as they say, is history!! On 9th July 1936, the sale was completed and the Bowater Years began.

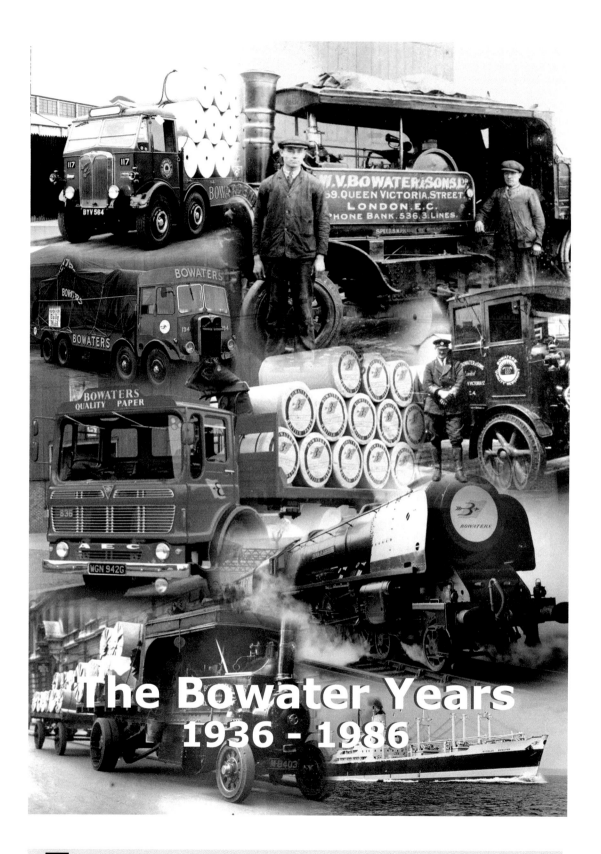

The Bowater Years
1936 - 1986

After the dinner meeting with Sir William Berry in July 1936, Sir Eric Bowater set about the task of bringing the Lloyd mills into the Bowater organisation. The process is recorded in detail in "Bowater – A History" by W. J. Reader and it was not without its problems.

Sir Eric Vansittart Bowater 1895-1962.

Whilst the Berrys had bought a solid business back in 1927, by 1936 the newspaper industry was finding it hard to make a profit – and Lloyds was no exception. Aside from this, was there another motive for the Berrys to rid themselves of the company?

They had certainly put a lot of money into the business and Gomer Berry had taken the title of Lord Kemsley. Unusually in a takeover situation, the Lloyds' assets were valued in 1935 at £6. 5m whilst the assets of all the Bowater companies around that time were only £4.9m. It was certainly unusual for one company to take control of another whose assets were significantly greater than their own.

The negotiations were lengthy and complicated. The major problem for Sir Eric was to find nearly £4.2m which was over 85% of the entire assets of the Bowater Group. However, by 9th July 1936 the deal had been struck and only 10 years after they started making newsprint, the Bowater Group had grown to become a group that was producing 500,000 tons of newsprint per year – 60% of all the newsprint manufactured in the UK. Added to this was the 45,000 tons of board, printing and wrapping papers produced at Sittingbourne.

So, more by chance than design, the Bowater-Lloyd group was born. At the Sittingbourne mills, many believed that it was Lloyds that had taken over Bowater but the transition was generally welcomed. But something more pressing was about to hit the headlines - a serious raw material crisis.

The Bowater Years 1936- 1986

The catalyst for this was summed up by Eric Bowater at the AGM of the Bowater's Paper Mills Ltd. In January 1938 as being "attributed to the operation of powerful foreign cartels of pulp exporters." This resulted in increases during 1937 of 77% for mechanical pulp (going from £4. 12. 6d to £8. 4. 0d per dry ton) and nearly 100% for sulphite pulp (from £8. 10. 0d to £16. 10. 0d per dry ton). A second factor was the growth in demand for wood products for the production of rayon. The newsprint manufacturer could not compete with this as there was greater added value in the making of rayon.

Coupled with this, Bowater had established fixed price contracts with most of the major newspapers. Some lengthy negotiations resulted in an increase from £10 to £11. 10s per ton, but even this was well below what was needed.

Despite this, The Chairman reported at the AGM that the Paper Mills Group had made a profit of £263,897 during the previous 12 months – an increase of £61,734 – but this fell short of what had been expected because of the increase in raw material costs.

Fortunately, the crisis was short lived and prices tumbled by July 1938 to below their 1936 average.

At the same time Bowater announced plans to concentrate the whole of the group's newsprint production to Kemsley, Northfleet and Mersey which allowed modernisation of Sittingbourne to take advantage of new markets. Among the classes of paper produced at Sittingbourne was Kraft Liner and they were manufacturing over 50, 000 tons per year. In addition, they had acquired the English rights of an American process for coating paper by an entirely new method – roll coating. The first roll coating machine for coated papers was installed on No. 11 machine and commenced manufacture in 1937. Soon No. 12 was modified for the same purpose.

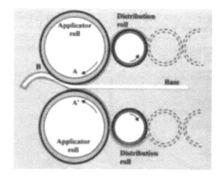

The Massey roll coater operated on-machine and coated both sides. Coating was poured between the metering rolls where it formed a puddle and was then metered down a series distribution rolls to the applicator roll. The latter were either rubber or chromium plated. The coatweight was about 12gsm.

This allowed Sittingbourne to develop new products and these were all grades of white printing paper with varying proportions of mechanical/sulphite pulps and would have been used for the letterpress and gravure markets. Initially the products of this machine went under the trade names Cotine 237 and Cotine 238. But by late 1938 another grade, Cotinex, had been introduced. This was described as "eminently suitable for superior classes of printing for which, normally, coated art paper would be employed. "

Cotine is described by the Paper Trades Review of 23rd March 1938 as "developed for inset and cover work. In colour and general appearance the new papers are very attractive and take colour very well. Cotine 237 is a middle grade and Cotine 238 the best grade. These qualities are also being made with a matt finish. "

From left to right: Len Jordan (Machine Foreman), Sid Weekes (Coater Man) and Nobby Elmer (Coater Dryerman) standing in front of the Massey coater unit on No. 11 machine. The rolls visible above their heads are the top set of coating metering rolls. The top (larger) applicator roll can just be seen to the left of these. The lower coating rolls are behind them. We know this is No. 11 machine and not No. 12 as the staging behind them is wooden and not metal.

Examples of packaging for Cotine and Cotinex

Referring to the trade depressions at the Annual Smoking Concert of the Mill Employees Sick Benefit Society in March 1937 (a bit of an anachronism here in today's world!), Mr. P.G. Denson, Vice Chairman of Bowaters-Lloyd Ltd., in his address said "You cannot avoid them but with the Lloyd motto of "Tails Up" I am quite sure we will be able to face them." In response, Mr. A.Clark, Vice Chairman of the Society, made reference to the large sum of money that had been spent at Sittingbourne. He went on to say "The new venture which we know today as Cotine has, I believe, more than realised expectations and it reflects great credit on those who have worked so hard to bring this about. To cope with the many orders, our ladies' staff has had to be more than doubled.

The gathering of Sittingbourne and Kemsley papermakers at the Mill Employees' Sick Benefit Society in 1937. Hundreds of employees, pensioners and visitors attended. The Society is still going strong in 2007 (Picture: East Kent Gazette).

"We have very clear evidence that our directors have the keenest interest in maintaining the upkeep of (Sittingbourne) mill against the changing conditions." The Sick Benefit Society was another example of the Lloyd policy of staff welfare having been set up in 1876. It still runs today (2007) with over 300 active members.

But the smooth running operation of the mill was shortly to be rudely interrupted by world events. In the lead up to the Second World War, demand for paper declined rapidly and this resulted in the closure of at least two paper machines at Sittingbourne. As many as 100 workers are reported to have been laid off although this was partly achieved by the retirement, with pension, of some 60 people over 65 years of age.

With the outbreak of war in 1939, the production of paper – and newspaper in particular – was curtailed even further, much of it as a result of Government controls.

But, during the Second World War, Sittingbourne Mill was able to turn its production over to support the war effort – as it had done for the Great War earlier. Bowater Lloyd was contracted by the Government to produce "Drop Tanks" and many types of munitions transport containers to carry shells for all sorts of artillery pieces.

The Drop Tanks enabled fighter escorts of the U.S.A.A.F to protect daylight bombers over a much wider range. The fighters would run on the tanks first which, once empty, would be jettisoned whilst they switched to internal fuel tanks.

Early in the war, these tanks were made from aluminium but as this became scarce, in 1943 Edward Lloyd Ltd. and Sittingbourne Mill were asked to design and make a paper and resin alternative.

Wartime production of a drop tank. The girl here seems to be chiselling away at the carcass to create a hole. Health & Safety would have a field day! Some part-finished carcasses can be seen in the background.

The tanks were very light (56lb.) and were fitted with a small explosive charge so that they could be destroyed once they were jettisoned. In this way, they doubled up as an incendiary device as they plummeted earthwards.

Undoubtedly, the production of these lightweight tanks in such quantities and in such a short time played a large part in the success of the American daylight bombing raids on Germany.

Reader's "Bowater - A History" records that, by the summer of 1945, Bowater had made 10,542,577 containers and other items from Kraft liner board, including 982,270 containers for 3.7 inch anti-aircraft shells, 8,324,612 for Bofors ammunition and 42,599 Jettison Drop Tanks. An interesting anecdote from Don Rouse, a former Sittingbourne employee who had been recruited to the Artillery, relates the story of an incident in Normandy. Artillery shells came packed in metal cases but were also protected by a cardboard tube. Picking out his shells one day he noticed that the

An exhibition of wartime material produced by the Bowater Group. To the right and behind are examples of the drop tanks produced at Sittingbourne. In the foreground is a Bofors gun and shells for this would have been protected with containers made by Bowater.

tubes were stamped "BL" – Bowater Lloyd. His reaction? "God – I wish I was back there!! "

A selection of the shell containers produced by Bowater during the war. Some of these would have been made in Sittingbourne.

A twelve inch scale model of one of Sittingbourne's drop tanks. (Model kindly loaned by Louise Harrison)

These two photographs show just some of the people that worked at the Mill during the war years. Some names are known but many have been lost over time. Pictures courtesy of Sittingbourne Heritage Museum.

1. Mr. White; 2. Mike Delane; 3. Reg Bush; 4. Bubbles Harlow; 5. Elsie Brown; 6. Edna Couchman (Mother in-law of Mick Clemons; 7. Joe Ford; 8. Bert Holness; 9. Gladys Bushrod (nee Hawkins)

During the 1950s, a number of significant steps were taken. Whilst straw continued to be used at Sittingbourne mill as a fibre source, it was limited to the coarser grades for conversion into corrugated rolls and boards. A new straw pulping plant included a bleaching stage which made the pulp a valuable material, used in combination with other pulps such as wood In the manufacture of fine, white printing papers. The plant had a capacity of 100 tonnes per week and provided the mill with the benefit of drawing on home grown straw, much of it from farms in the South East.

An example of bales of straw being offloaded at Ridham. This material may have come from Iberia where Frank Lloyd had been prudent in the setting up of exclusive supply deals.

Once off-loaded, the straw bales would have been transported along an overhead conveyor to the Sittingbourne Mill store. At some points along this route – mainly near the Kemsley end– relics of the original concrete pillars can still be seen (2007).

These "strawstacks" would have been built up behind the mill. This board on the front of this one shows that it was completed on 6/6/52 and comprises 9270 bales.

In 1950 a new straw cutter was installed at Sittingbourne.

At the top right of this shot can be seen a number of "strawstacks". This area is now the retail park (2007). The old straw storage sheds are rear left in the picture but it is not thought that these were being used for this purpose at this time. The small "scaffold" centre left is being used to offload reels from a railway truck so the sheds are probably being used for reel storage. The houses in the foreground have long since been demolished. This picture is clearly post 1957 as it has been taken from the water tower which was only completed in that year.

As part of the Bowater "Master Plan for Expansion" announced by Chairman Eric Bowater in May 1955, a new Power Plant was built at Kemsley allowing the old-fashioned and uneconomical one at Sittingbourne to close down. At a cost of £2.5m, this resulted in a saving of 50,000 tonnes of coal a year and was the most modern and efficient in Europe. To feed the new power station, a new Jetty was built and a mile long conveyor was installed to take fuel direct from the holds of the colliers to the coal store adjoining the boiler house.

A two and a half mile steam pressure surface main, at that time the longest in Britain, was built to link the Kemsley power station and the mill at Sittingbourne. To allow for expansion, the piping was laid in a snake like pattern and the main therefore required a track some 30 to 40 feet wide throughout its length. The main followed the route of the existing railway link, which was to continue to be used to carry material to the mill until 1969.

Part of the conveyor system used to carry coal to the mill. This is the wharf end as the Ridham cranes can just be seen in the background.

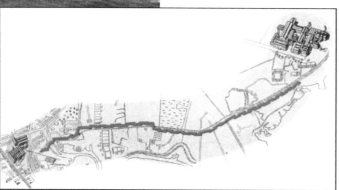

A plan of the steam surface main published in "The World Watches Bowater" in 1956. The "zig-zag" route of the main can be seen clearly and follows the line of the railway. Some of the railway ran on a viaduct along its route as did the steam main.

The 1950s also saw the demand for roll coated paper expand with the rise in literacy and cultural standards and two new supercalenders were installed to improve the printing surface of these papers. Around this time, the Lithocote grade was introduced being designed for printing by the lithographic process which was now challenging the more traditional letterpress.

In the Annual Report of 1950, it was reported that Sittingbourne had embarked on an Anglo American venture with Bowater-Riegel Corp. to produce glassine paper. By 1953, the conversion of No. 15 machine for the production of glassine and greaseproof paper had been completed. After 1957, much of the kraft production had been transferred from Sittingbourne to Ellesmere Port. At this point in its history, Sittingbourne Mill produced a greater variety of products than any other Bowater Mill.

Roll Coated papers produced at Sittingbourne were widely used for the printing of illustrated trade journals and magazines.

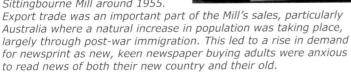

The Despatch Department at Sittingbourne Mill around 1955. Export trade was an important part of the Mill's sales, particularly Australia where a natural increase in population was taking place, largely through post-war immigration. This led to a rise in demand for newsprint as new, keen newspaper buying adults were anxious to read news of both their new country and their old.

Whilst on the subject of variety of products, the 1962 issue of "Paper Makers' and Merchants' Directory of All Nations" published by Business Publications Limited London lists Sittingbourne as makers of Woodfree & Mechanical Printings, Banks & Bonds, "Postscript" Bond, "Postscript" Duplicator, Cartridge Papers, Roll coated Papers, Bleached Boards, Sack & Unglazed Kraft, Straw Paper and Wrapping Papers. The Directory lists Sittingbourne as having 8 machines "one 80 in., one 116 in., one 128 in., one 138 in., one 140 in., one 156 in., two 162 in., one lamination machine 78 in."

By 1966, the same Directory entry has changed slightly with products itemised as Woodfree Printings, Mechanical Printings, Postscript Bond & Duplicator, Postilion, Cartridge, G.I.P., Bleached Board, Blade Coated & Roll Coated papers, Container, Sack & Unglazed Kraft, Absorbent Kraft, Chipboard, Straw & Wrapping Papers. Now, there were only 6 machines recorded "one 113 in., one 128 in., one 140 in., one 158 in., two 160 in., one laminator 78 in., one off-machine Blade Coater 160 in."

1957 also saw the completion of the water tower which was to remain a landmark throughout the surrounding area. Designed and built by Bierrum & Partners of Harrow, London, the foundations were started in July 1956 and the tower was "topped out" in March 1957. At 117ft. 6ins. high, the tower could hold 100,000 gallons of water. A total of 40 piles were driven, each 20ft. long and with a maximum working load of 35 tons each.

Laying the foundations, 3rd July 1956.

The tower was constructed from reinforced concrete and is designed to withstand the maximum wind loading.

At least one worker fell off the scaffolding during construction but by some divine intervention he came out of it with only cuts and bruises and was taken back up the tower so that he did not lose his head for heights!

27th September 1956

Nearing completion 6th February 1957.

Publisher's note:
The tower was demolished on 9th Sept 2012.

The Development of Jubilee Street

Situated as it is near the middle of the town, Sittingbourne Mill has always had limited opportunities for expanding but even back as far as 1938 the need to create more space was recognised. Proposals were drawn up for the closure of Jubilee Street at the rear of the Mill and building a new finishing house. For whatever reason, these plans were not immediately carried out but in February 1956, a site survey plan drawn up by Mears Bros. of Sydenham showed that the houses in the street had already been demolished to make way for the new building.

The old firing range, however remained in place and would still have been in use by the mill's shooting club. Construction must have commenced in the late 1950's or early 1960's as another plan of 29th December 1961 now shows the completed building.

Taken from an early 1950's aerial shot (pre water tower), this shows that the houses in Jubilee Street have already been demolished. The rifle range is still visible just above the demolished area in the centre left. Charlotte Street runs along the top of the picture. Regis Road can be seen running from the top centre towards the mill.

This drawing, dated June 1938 outlines an early plan for the closure of Jubilee Street and part of Regis Road. It is actually titled "Plan of Cottage Property in the Precincts of Sittingbourne belonging to B. L.P & P. M.Ltd." (Bowater Lloyd Pulp & Paper Mill Ltd.) The houses in Jubilee Street are already described as "Pulled Down" but this was not actually carried out until much later.

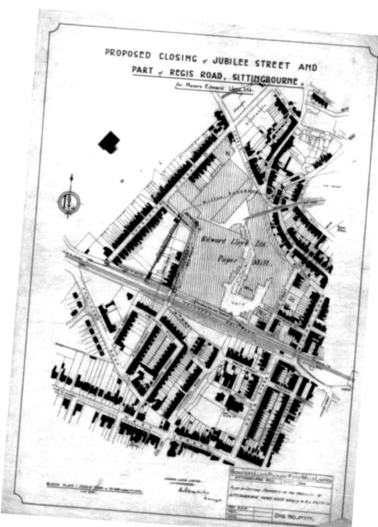

Artist's impression of new supercalender house as published in Bowater World April 1961.

The History of Sittingbourne Mill

Having pioneered roll coating in the 1930's, Bowater now turned its attention to the latest coating technology – trailing blade coating. In the early 1960's, a group of Research Technicians travelled the world and brought back much information on the blade coating of mechanical (groundwood) papers but virtually nothing was known about coating of the woodfree (chemical) papers that were being produced at Sittingbourne at the time. This was their challenge and the Mill had to learn the hard way!

Whilst the trailing blade process was a British invention, it had been developed commercially in the USA but this was to be the first of its type in the UK. At a cost of £1.25m, six separate stages were involved, all of them large and complex construction jobs. One of the paper machines had to be almost entirely rebuilt to make the best quality base paper for coating. A new plant had to be installed for preparing the specially formulated coating mix. The new coater – the heart of the process – was in itself a major construction job.

The coater fully installed

A Finishing house was erected to accommodate a purpose built high speed supercalender plus new winding machines. Finally, a new Cutter House and Salle was needed to cope with the big increase in output. "Our biggest problem, " said Mill Manager Clive Saunders "was the merging of the blade coating operation within the limitations imposed by existing buildings and land."

An article in the Electrical Times of 29th August 1963 describes in great detail the latest of many Bowater innovations – blade coating. The first of its kind in the UK, the "trailing blade" coater had by that time been in production for over 18 months. The control gear for the coater is described as "extremely complex, with no less than 80 control functions having to be correct before the machine can be started". The article also refers to the "novelty of a flying splice that can join paper at full speed of 2000 feet per minute (600m/min.)"

Leslie Walledge (Mill Superintendent), Jack O'Regan (Chief Engineer), Clive Saunders (Manager) and Bob Fosbraey (Coaterman)

So, Bowater pioneered blade coating in the UK as an advanced, fast and economical process, producing a paper having a finish far superior to the roll coated grades produced until this time. This product, first marketed as B. 21, was the best of both worlds – it had a printable quality challenging that of a good "brush" coated but sold at little more than a standard "machine" coated. B. 21 was first developed for the letterpress and gravure markets but was later adapted for offset lithography. To complete the range, Bowater introduced B. 22 for catalogues and B. 23 for printing from a continuous reel.

Later the trade name was changed and "Beaublade" was born!!

Whilst demand for coated papers increased, newsprint – one of the other main products from Sittingbourne - declined, partly because of reduced EFTA tariffs and increased competition from Scandinavia. As a result of this, Sir Christopher Chancellor, the then Chairman of Bowater, announced in 1964 that two of the eight paper machines at Sittingbourne would close.

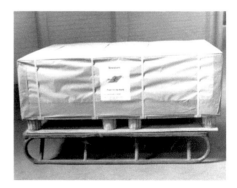

Examples of packaging for Beaublade 20 Cartridge and Beaublade 21 Offset from the 1960's. The Beaublade label on the right is for 1000 sheets of 140 gsm size 1016 x 1549mm, thought to be for the French market.

In 1966, in keeping with its innovative outlook, Bowater embarked on a three year project to introduce computer control to the manufacturing processes. It was the Americans who made the first attempts at computer control in the late 1950's/early 1960's but with very limited success. It took a small British company – Wolvercote Mill – to show that such a system could work and the challenge was taken up by three of the, at that time, major UK paper manufacturers – Reeds, Wiggins Teape and Bowater.

PM16 and its associated stock preparation plant at Sittingbourne were selected by Bowater Research for the project. The long term plan was to extend this to include No. 17 machine, the blade coater and the supercalender. So, Sittingbourne was a pioneer in the UK in a project that was to change the history of papermaking for ever.

Bowater Project Manager Don Attwood saw the possibilities and inspired the purchase. In an article in Bowater World, Attwood described " …. a lack of uniformity in the substance and quality of the paper meant that the mill was giving away fibre! " Introduction of computer control would achieve uniformity plus a reduction in the time taken to change from one grade to another. A winning formula all round!

These two pictures show the computer components being delivered into the mill over the wall in Church Street.

In a later interview, Rod Morley, Sittingbourne's man on Attwood's team reported that this was "…. a long term project and one that took over 5 years of my working life!" Various computer firms were invited to make studies. The AEI approach, their men and their software were preferred.

The computer contained about 100 control loops from the simple to the complex The majority were complex i.e. they interacted and their job was to control the basis weight, moisture, formation, blending and consistency. The simple ones controlled chest levels, flows, temperatures and pressures. By 1969, such progress had been made and the main objective of better process control had been achieved that the project was hailed as a world leader. A World Symposium on Paper Machine Control taking place in Oxford that year sought the opportunity for their 50 or so delegates to visit Sittingbourne to see the success of the project at first hand.

For the technically minded the computer was described as a "CON/PAC 4060 with 16K of 24 bit word store." By today's (2007) standards this is a fraction of the power of the smallest laptop! It was somewhat unreliable as well so full automatic standby control facilities had to be introduced to take over in the event of computer failure.

Now taken for granted, computer technology in those days was "leading edge" but was played down by Attwood as "…. contrary to popular belief, not a piece of equipment that can only be handled by mathematicians in white coats! It is there for use by the men concerned with the immediate practical problems of making and preparing stock and paper."

Programme for the World Symposium on Paper Machine Control held at Sittingbourne on 19th September 1969.

Bill Whitehead and Harry Cyprus at the controls of the massive computer alongside No.16 machine which can just be seen through the window on the right. A simple laptop would do the same job 100 times over today!

Rod Morley, Sittingbourne's man on the team, and Fred Mantle check the readings on the control panel beside No. 16 machine.

Fred Mantle & Harry Cyprus examining a data printout.

Despite being a trailblazer in its day, the system was far from ideal and did not give the expected savings in cost. Over the years this "dinosaur" technology was replaced by the developments of companies such as Measurex who introduced a user-friendly TV screen to the digital computer technology and were far more specialised and geared to the paper industry. By the mid 1970's, computer control systems became well established and a striking tribute to the Measurex systems installed by then came in 1975 from Jack Earle, Machineman on No. 17. "It's like giving a blind man eyes for the first time" he said!!

The same Bowater World article of 1969 reports the installation of two Masson Scott Thrisell cutters, each costing £100,000, capable of running much faster than their predecessors but more accurately and with less dust and debris. This technology was the beginning of the end for the Salle operations as now Bowater were able to send paper "free of joins, variations and rubbish" without always going through the Salle.

Jack Earle, Machineman on No.17 in the 1970s

Views of one of the Masson Scott cutters installed in 1969.

The Salle Operation

The Salle was a very important part of the Mill's operation as every pallet coming from the cutters had to be checked for faults and defects – a very necessary role in those days. It was the last port of call before the customer and no pallets left the mill before going to the Salle. Once sorted, the sheets would be counted and the paper would go for bulk packing or stay in the Salle where it would be ream wrapped.

In the 1950's, there were 10 cutters producing maybe 1 pallet an hour so the Salle was a very labour intensive area. At its peak, Sittingbourne had four Salle areas and would have employed in excess of 200 people, mainly women. It could take the Salle girl most of her working day to sift through just one pallet and as much as 50% of the paper would be rejected! Ream wrapping a pallet may have taken an hour. Porters were employed to remove rejected paper, move pallets in and out and apply labels or stencil the packaging.

View of No. 1 Salle thought to be from the 1950s.

Initial Inspection of the pallet. The girl would fan and inspect the top sheets and the general appearance of the stack. If it was deemed OK it would go straight forward for packing.

Arthur Simpson, former Burmese Policeman, who worked as a Salle Porter during the 1960s.

In 1982, when no. 15 machine shut, as many as 50 Salle girls were amongst the 250 who were made redundant. Over the next few years, as production increased and quality improved, the need for the Salle reduced and it went into decline and the operation was eventually closed.

Jean Wildish seen sorting for faults. After the initial inspection, each sheet on the pallet would be hand sorted against a "bracket". Here, the rejected sheets are being put on the trestle to the right.

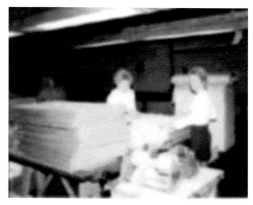

With the sheets now sorted, they would be counted prior to packing.

Salle Girls packing reams by hand - 1975. Deanne Wood (left) and Pamela Amos in No1 Salle. (Picture courtesy of Alan Amos)

A Century of Continuous Papermaking

The Spring 1976 Issue of Bowlines was dubbed "Sittingbourne Centenary Issue" to commemorate 100 years of continuous papermaking on the site. It was in 1876 that Edward Lloyd announced at a public dinner in the Bull Hotel that the largest papermaking machine in the UK would be making paper on a continuous basis that year. Just five years later, another young man – William Vansittart Bowater – set up as a general paper merchant in the City of London.

It is a remarkable fact that the paths of these two great men then ran almost parallel, each founding what was the largest paper organisation in the UK and the two finally coming together in what was to be one of the largest organisations of its kind in the world.

This wonderful cartoon depicting papermaking in light hearted style is by artist Leigh Taylor and was commissioned for use on the cover of Bowlines.

Edward Lloyd   *William Vansittart Bowater*

Over the next 15 years or so, changes continued throughout the mill. One highly significant change was the introduction of the Nimrod range of coated papers – the name is believed to be the brainchild of an ex-RAF Marketing Manager, taking it from the reconnaissance aircraft that first flew in the early 1970's. Nimrod was the next generation of blade coated papers, replacing Beaublade in 1973 and continuing as the flagship brand of Sittingbourne Mill right up until its closure.

Stripped out and ready for the rebuild.

Looking into the side of the coater from the instrument panel. On the left is Bert Fosbraey with coaterman George Bolton.

Graham Harrison (left) and Bob Fosbraey (Engineer)

Around the same time, the roll coated grades were rebranded as Buccaneer – another RAF connection.

In 1978, the coater was completely rebuilt to introduce new coating heads and improved drying, both of which enabled higher coat weights to be applied with a degree of precision and reproducibility not previously attainable.

This was in response to the demands for a paper with the reproduction of high gloss art but without the reflected glare. Nimrod Matt Art was the result.

The puddle coating heads were replaced by the very latest design of Beloit inverted coating heads, chosen so that both blade angle and blade loading could be varied independently and "on the run". New drying equipment was also needed.

Two of the original four Gardner air caps were removed and four Overly air foil dryers installed. The coater rebuild was completed in only five weeks.

Described as a "remarkable revolution", in 1980 Sittingbourne converted from an "acid" to an "alkali" mill. Alum and rosin sizes were replaced with synthetic materials which enabled the introduction of chalk as a filler. Chalk was cheaper than clay and could be used at higher levels which reduced the use of costly fibre.

The initial trials were on No. 17 machine and Technical Manager Ron Vincent explained what was involved in the July 1981 issue of Bowlines. "It meant a completely different approach to the chemistry of the wet end. It meant a switch to the single addition of a synthetic sizing agent. Running a neutral size machine also keeps the system cleaner so there are fewer expensive breaks resulting from dirt and sludge. "

But it was not all plain sailing. Said Mill Superintendent Frank Ryde "it was one of those blood, sweat and tears situations – and once started, you've got to see it through! "

The result was a paper with better finish, better bulk and better gloss – The Nimrod Premier range.

"The pursuit of excellence" was the theme for the launch of this new range. Included in the portfolio of products was one brand new product, another so dramatically improved as to make it virtually a new grade and three well established grades.

The evolution of the Nimrod logo.

The new paper was Nimrod Super Art, a double coated sheet for the high quality market with strong visible characteristics of brightness, gloss and surface smoothness. The improved grade was New Nimrod Art, formerly Nimrod Art whilst Nimrod Matt Art, Nimrod Cartridge and Nimrod Web Art remained the established products.

This range continued to be supported by Buccaneer Matt and SC, the economy coated sheets.

Tom Usher, Frank Ryde, Barry Butler and Ronald Downes.

Examples of advertising material for Nimrod Super Art. The promotion used hitherto unseen photographs taken by mountaineer Chris Bonnington including his ascent of the South Ridge of Mount Kongur in China and the East Ridge of Mount Cook in New Zealand.

Business took a turn in 1982 which was reported as "probably one of the worst years in the British papermaking industry" by then General Manager John Goodwin. The reasons were cited as too much coated paper capacity, reduced demand as a result of the recession, improved quality of imported product and falling prices. This meant the closure of No. 15 machine and four cutters and the loss of about 280 jobs.

John Goodwin

During 1984 and 1985, major changes took place as part of the "Wharf Transfer Plan" which was designed to allow the sale of storage areas at the creek and move storage to the mill. Hailed at the time as "the most significant and radical changes in 20 years" this involved a great deal of structural alteration, re-siting and upgrading of machinery and equipment, plus improvements to production flow lines and handling methods.

Pre-winders were moved from the coater floor to a previously derelict area on the first floor, later to include No. 1 coater. Jumbo reel racking was installed in the blade coater house to provide better storage for machine reels prior to coating. Cutters 6, 9 & 10 were dismantled and re-located.

The crane for the prewinder house being lowered into position. The erection took 3 days and a 50 ton crane to heave the structure into place.

Before and after……..! The prewinder house has been transformed from the empty shell above to a smart, new unit in just 3 months. Ray Kite, Finishing Foreman (left), and Ted Smith, Finishing Superintendent, view the changes.

Monty August, Managing Director, stated in Bowlines of 1984 that these changes were part of "...our long term aim to make improvements which will give Sittingbourne Mill an opportunity to become more competitive. At the same time we will continue to improve the quality of our products." He also reported that No. 14 machine had moved away from just producing paper for corrugated cases to production of core paper and board, roofing felt base and dyed chipboard.

Alan Tumber at the new Pasaban.

With their final outer wrap, the narrow reels are now ready for despatch to be wound into cardboard tubes.

The wide reel has now been slit into a large number of very narrow reels and is being stretch wrapped for ultimate protection by Steve Sidders.

"Down The Tube" was an article published in the December 1984 issue of Bowlines and describes how the paper for cardboard tubes was cut and packed. A Pasaban Coiler costing £80,000 was installed in the rewinder bay. The Pasaban takes a large reel of brown paper, about 1300mm wide and cuts it into small webs, some of which can be just 76mm wide. These are then spirally wound on a shaft to give the inner cores for such items as silver foil, paper toweling and toilet paper.

Also in 1984, some highly sophisticated control equipment was installed on Nos. 16 & 17

machines, including a brand new Measurex system and computer controlled slice rods on PM17. Meanwhile, the first remote crane controls were introduced in the coater house. This meant that the crane drivers left their cabs and "…. were firm footed on the ground with an infra red control box the size of a transistor radio. " (Bowlines August 1984)

The December 1984 issue of Bowlines reported another significant development – the first ever working during the traditional summer shut period. This was undertaken as an experiment and was considered a great success.

Investment in machinery continued into 1985 and by December of that year, the blade coater had undergone a £400,000 refit which included improved infra red drying. One of the bottlenecks at that time was the supercalender which could not keep pace with the demand for Nimrod smooth grade. The installation of the on-line calender on the coater relieved this problem.

The Kusters Mat-on-line (MOL) was another technological first for Sittingbourne, being the first European installation of a tandem calender on a blade coating line. The printing properties of Nimrod Smooth improved significantly and General Manager, Barry Butler, reported, "Broke fell by 50% and a production stage i. e. supercalendering was cut out. Coater throughput also increased with speeds now reaching 850m/min."

Bob Carrol, blade coater foreman and Derek Norris, 2nd coaterman, on the matt-on-line installation.

The Bowater Years 1936- 1986

The most notable investment in 1985/6 was the extension of the main entrance and car park. Stage 1 required the demolition of the old Personnel building in Westbourne Street. Staff in the building were relocated to the main administration building giving them greater accessibility to staff in the mill.

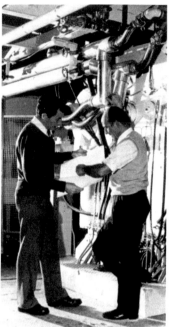

Lesley Glover, Don Oakes, Tracy Bevan and Aubrey Maryott settle in to their new offices.

Ron Vincent, Coating Manager discusses a fine point with Bob Carrol.

In Stage 2 in 1986, the 1950's cottage property opposite reception was demolished along with the splendid historic 10ft. high gates. In its time the cottage had been used to house some mill employees and also as an ambulance room.

By removing the narrow gates, two large vehicles were now able to pass each other with ease. The area between the mill buildings and the road was laid as a car park. A line of fir trees was planted by the Milton Road railway bridge and along the railway embankment to provide a pleasant green screen for the parking area.

In 2007, just a few days before the mill shut, at least one of these – now more than 30ft. tall - was blown down in a very severe gale, unfortunately causing extensive damage to a contractor's car!

This section of a 1960's aerial shot shows the old Personnel Office building to the left of the car park in Westbourne Street before it was demolished to allow extension of the car park.

The beautiful old wrought iron gate at the mill entrance before it was removed to allow expansion of the parking area.

And after – with the gate removed and the cottage demolished.

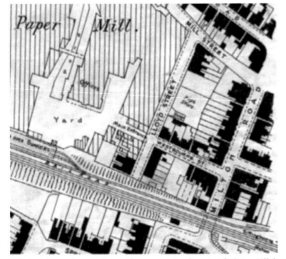

With both the personnel offices and the cottage gone, the car park was significantly extended.

This plan shows how the area in front of the mill looked in 1938. The mill entrance was then in Lloyd Street but by 1986 the whole area between this and Milton Road had been demolished to create the new car park.

Monty August

In the August 1986 issue of Bowlines, Monty August reviewed these investment plans totalling some £5m that had taken place over the past three years. Sittingbourne Mill had been transformed into a profitable and efficient operation with a product range capable of competing in the UK marketplace. Nimrod Gloss was now available in sheet form; the new matt-on-line on the coater had enabled the Mill to produce Nimrod Smooth; the Milton Economy range was introduced to fight low price foreign competition.

No. 14 machine continued to be the best producer in the UK for core centres for toilet rolls, cling film and the like. In summing up, Monty warned of the increasing competition from new European mills. "We are not frightened by the situation" he said "but it is important that we know what we've got to face. We certainly can't sit back or relax. We have planned an investment programme for the next three years involving changes and improvements in most areas. "

No doubt in the back of his mind was the impending changes in the mill ownership.

For, in November 1986, Tom Wilding Chairman and Managing Director of Bowaters U.K. Paper Company announced in Bowlines "Now it's our company! " In his message he welcomed the introduction of a new era. "We are no longer part of a large group. We don't have to worry anymore that a faceless concern might take us over. For the first time we can get on with our job of making and selling paper without looking over our shoulders. "

Sittingbourne Paper Company Ltd. was about to be born.

Evolution of the site from the air and the ground during the Bowater Years

Taken in the 1950's before the water tower was built. In the centre foreground, Westbourne Street is still built up and there is no car park. The houses in Jubilee Street at the rear of the mill have been demolished in preparation for the mill extension which was not completed until 1961. To the right, the houses in the Church Street area can still be seen.

The Peace and Plenty pub opposite the mill entrance in Westbourne Street

A closer view of Westbourne Street

The 1980's. The water tower is now in place and the housing around the Westbourne Street entrance have been demolished to make way for the car park. The Jubilee Street extension at the rear is complete.

Also the 1980's, but from a different direction. The old straw sheds (centre left) can still be seen and these were being used as a reel storage area (Nicholls yard).

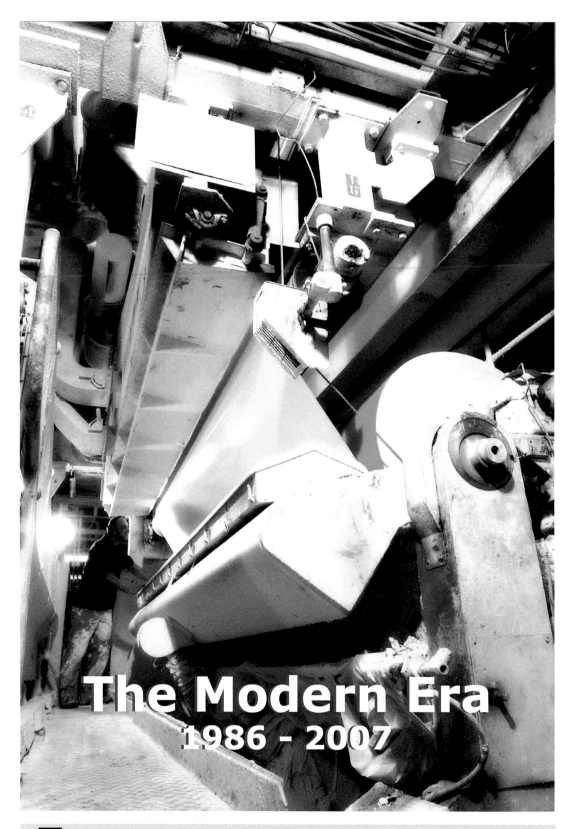

The Modern Era
1986 - 2007

After more than 100 years of stability with only two owners, the final 20 years leading up to the closure in 2007 were turbulent by comparison with no less than three owners exerting their influence on the mill. The birth of Sittingbourne Paper Company was the result of a very successful Management Buy-out. An article in the November 1988  issue of Acquisitions Monthly explains how it came about. The seeds for this were sown when Bowater Industries decided in the mid 1980's to sever connections with the pulp and paper industries. Tom Wilding, then Chairman of UK Paper plc, and four of his senior managers offered to buy the British papermaking and merchanting businesses.

They succeeded in doing this with their own capital, that of 70 other managers and the help of Electra and Scandinavian Bank plc. On the 19th September 1986, they bought Britain's largest papermaking company for £38m with four mills, a capacity approaching 500,000 tonnes and one of the largest UK paper merchants. All the institutions involved reacted so quickly that the whole transformation was structured and the purchase effected in only eight weeks. Based on the previous year's profits of £1.4m on sales of £154m, some pundits thought Bowater had the best of the deal. But Tom Wilding knew that the years of hard work that his frustrated but dedicated team had put in transforming a newsprint company into a modern high quality printing and writing group was about to pay off. With a highly motivated management team, 2,400 enthusiastic employees and the support of Electra and Scandinavian Bank, Wilding set about renaming the company as UK Paper plc and arranging its refinancing and a flotation within 15 months.

Tom Wilding was only 14 when he entered the paper industry, joining his local mill in Walthamstow. This mill became part of Bowater Scott, the tissue producers. During the 1950's and early 1960's he worked his way up, becoming manager of their Northfleet Mill, one of the largest tissue mills in Europe. During the mid 1960's, Wilding joined Bowater at their large newsprint mill at Ellesmere Port. Within a short period he was appointed Mill Director with the brief to return the mill to profit, which he did successfully.

At this time Bowater was heavily committed to British newsprint manufacture with 16 of its paper machines producing more than 500,000 tonnes per annum for Fleet Street and the provincial press. In the early 1970's, Wilding was charged with devising a strategy plan for Bowater's UK newsprint operations. It was at this point, as a member of the main Bowater Board and Chairman of UK Paper plc that he recognised the need to concentrate on added value products.

The flotation would have taken place in 1987 but was delayed because of the October share crash. Finally, on 19th March 1988, the offer for sale took place and was one of the first new issues after the October crash. Eleven times over-subscribed at the offer price of 135p, the flotation valued the company at £105m. Wilding was particularly keen to see his employees participate in the share issue so a generous matching share offer was arranged. Almost half of the employees took advantage of the offer. Even during the protracted flotation negotiations, there were other issues to be resolved. The one difficult area was the Kemsley site which Wilding described as "the curate's egg".

The New Thames Mill was an excellent investment but the Kemsley Mill was unprofitable. Wilding concluded a complex deal with D. S.Smith to sell the Kemsley Mill, its associated waste paper business and to set up on the site a joint venture company to supply essential services to both companies – Grovehurst Energy. The management team believed that this was a logical move because they lacked the in-house packaging paper converting capacity. It also meant that they could focus on their strategy of moving out of newsprint into higher added value products, especially quality printing papers.

On 12th January 1988, the name of the company was changed from B. U.K. Paper (Holdings) Limited to UK Paper Limited, comprising Sittingbourne Paper Company Limited, The Donside Paper Company Limited, New Thames Paper Company Limited and William Guppy and Son Limited. The new company was firmly established as the leading printing and writing paper manufacturers in the United Kingdom.

Commenting at the time, Tom Wilding said, "this is the end of the Bowater UK story. After 40 years with Bowater it is a bitter sweet moment for me, but this is the beginning of a very exciting future. "

In his first review as Managing Director of the newly formed Sittingbourne Paper Company Ltd, Monty August, in the 1988 Report & Accounts, welcomed the fact that "Demand for both coated woodfree and packaging papers remained very strong throughout 1988 and Sittingbourne Paper enjoyed a very successful year with improvements in trading profit of 20%, an increase in turnover of 14% and a 10% increase  of sales tonnage. "During the year we continued to upgrade plant within the paper mill, particularly that associated with computer measurement and control, the preparation of raw materials and the equipment for cutting paper into sheets. In addition, we completed the commissioning of a new winder and a new headbox for one of our paper machines."

He also revealed for the first time that a new machine for coated woodfree paper was to be installed early in 1990. But before that, there were other developments that were to have a significant impact on the mill.

Peter Hadler studying one of the modern Measurex computer control screens in 1986

In the late 1980's, a high proportion of coated woodfree papers imported into the UK were double coated and Sittingbourne saw an opportunity to enter this market. The decision was taken to install a second blade coater to apply a pre-coat to the base paper.

The choice was between an off-machine coater or an on-machine Billblade unit. The off-machine option would give the mill greater flexibility to continue to supply the wide range of grades required by the UK market and this was the route chosen. The precoater was installed in 1989 and enabled the mill to produce single, double or triple coated products. These investments in coating technology were made alongside changes on the paper machine and the end result was Nimrod 2.

Nimrod 2 - a new generation of double and triple coated papers in gloss, smooth and cartridge qualities. The range was quickly accepted in the marketplace for its high ink lift and clean, crisp reproduction. It brought Sittingbourne papers to a new level.

No.1 Precoater

 # FLETCHER CHALLENGE

Then, in 1990, the second phase of Sittingbourne's new ownership changes took place when the company was taken over by Fletcher Challenge, a New Zealand based company. Fletcher Challenge was the result of a merger between three long-established New Zealand companies – Fletcher Holdings, Challenge Corporation and Tasman Pulp and Paper.

When the company officially opened for business on January 5th 1981, it was the biggest company on the New Zealand stock exchange judged by the value of its shares. Fletchers was a conglomerate strong in construction and manufacturing; Challenge had made money from its interests in dairy farms, grazing land and orchards; Tasman was the odd one out, being a powerful force in the pulp and paper industry. During its early years, Fletcher Challenge embarked on what it called an operation to purchase "sizeable offshore positions. "

The first of these was in early 1983, paying NZ$421m for Crown Zellerbach in Canada. Just a few years later and UK Paper fell to the company's chequebook. The £312m purchase was the group's first move into Europe's highly competitive pulp and paper market.

Membership of this group provided the mill with access to a wide range of new materials, manufacturing, financial and management resources.

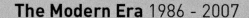

The PM15 Project

Sittingbourne Mill then embarked on the project that was to change the face of the mill for ever – the installation of PM15.

This project was the culmination of some five years of preparation, meticulous planning and co-ordination to ensure that there was no disruption to the mill's output during the construction process. PM16 and PM17 continued to provide base stock for the full range of coated papers and PM14 continued to produce packaging grades.

Designed and manufactured by Sulzer Escher Wyss, this machine was the first purpose-built, fine-coated paper machine to be built in the UK – another first for Sittingbourne Paper. To prepare the way for this machine, virtually every key piece of production equipment had to be replaced or rebuilt over the previous years.

As well as the precoater installation and the addition of the matt-on-line on the top coater, changes were made to the existing paper machines, including considerable wet end modifications.

The site in the early days of construction. The old 15 machine has been removed and PM14 is still running to the left of the picture – and continued to run throughout.

The finishing processes were greatly improved through the rebuilding of the supercalenders, adding temperature controlled rolls and softened water. Two of the winders were replaced with a Jagenberg single drum winder and a third was rebuilt at a cost of £740,000. To complete the investment, a new state of the art Jagenberg sheeter was added to the conversion department and increased sheeting capacity to 55,000 tonnes a year.

The next phase was to remove the old PM15 which had been shut in 1982. New structural work included the driving of new piles to accommodate the weight of the new machine. During the construction a major fire destroyed the existing roof which had

The new roof steel work looking from PM14 side. After the unplanned fire a temporary roof of corrugated iron and tarpaulin was put in place to protect PM14 and the construction site from the elements.

been due for removal anyway so, until the new roof was completed work had to carry on exposed to the elements!!

By July 1990, the wire and press sections had been completed; by August the drying section, hoods, instrumentation and control systems had been installed and some initial testing had been carried out. By October the machine was running.

View from the dry end. In the foreground is the reel drum and behind this is the winder floor pulper.

Two views of the PM15 soleplates in place viewed from the dry end. PM14 continues to run to the right.

Looking down from the roof at the wet end. The press section is now in place.

The job is nearly complete. The Dandy Roll is in place and the machine is up and running. All that remains is for the marble floor tiles to be laid.

Throughout all this work, PM14 continued to run – even after the roof had been destroyed – and it is a testament to the dedication of the crews that this was possible. Once PM15 was fully commissioned, PM14 was removed and production of packaging grades was transferred to PM17. PM15 came on stream at a crucial time; with the introduction of the single European Market in 1992, demand for coated woodfree papers increased and Sittingbourne Mill was in a position to compete with its European rivals.

Investment continued in the next few years. Installations included a new twin drum winder (1991), a stretchwrap machine for reel packing (1992), a new Bielomatic cutter and Bielomatic ream packer (1994).

Bielomatic cutter

Stretchwrap

In the mid 1990's, Fletcher Challenge embarked on another major project with UK Paper which was the design, development and construction of the UK's most technically advanced paper recycling plant. Fletcher Challenge had a policy of sourcing cellulose fibre locally for their manufacturing plants to reduce dependency on imported material. With no local source of wood fibre available and pressure to recycle increasing, the conditions were ideal for the project.

At a cost of around £43m, the plant commenced production in 1996 and was soon to be producing arguably the best quality recycled fibre in the world. There was no immediate impact for Sittingbourne Mill as the fibre was for use at Kemsley for the production of uncoated papers. However, by 1997, there

was a project to complement the uncoated grades with a coated grade from Sittingbourne.

EVOLVE Coated was the result made from 100% recycled fibre. But the lack of experience of producing recycled paper at Sittingbourne resulted in a number of problems. Firstly, the strength of the paper was compromised; then dirt contamination from the recycled fibre built up in the stock preparation system with the result that all products, including Nimrod, became contaminated and prone to dirt spots. EVOLVE Coated was not a success but the lessons learnt then and by Kemsley led to a very different result in 2006 with the emergence of Era Silk. (See later)

In May 1995, Sittingbourne Mill embarked on yet another first for the UK paper industry. After almost five years of successful running, the size press on PM15 was replaced by a film press - or Symsizer to use its trade name.

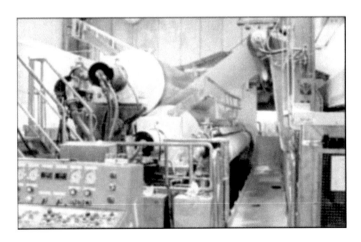

Nothing revolutionary perhaps except that Sittingbourne had decided to use the film press to apply a first layer of coating rather than a starch size. At that time, no other mill in the UK was doing this and it was still in its infancy in the USA. The application of up to 10gsm of coating to each side of the base paper gave a much improved surface for the top coat. This allowed the mill to consolidate its position as a leader in the production of double coated art papers. The procedure had the added benefit of giving better runnability by reducing the number of web breaks that were associated with size press technology.

As the decade continued, a new corporate identity was established (1996) and the refurbishment of the reception area completed which included the building of a new frontage.

The imposing new Visitor Centre with its strong Greco-Roman influence.

John Ollard of the identity project team said in 1996, "We chose this design for a number of reasons. The colours blue and orange are reminiscent of the European Union flag and reflect the fact that we are an international company.

We also liked the fact that the design was smart and contemporary without being gimmicky. We believe that we have achieved the stylish, dynamic image which staff told us they wanted."

By the end the decade, the mill went through yet another change of ownership. In 1999, the Finnish Company Metsa Serla took control and Sittingbourne Mill was now part of one of the largest paper manufacturing groups in Europe. Metsa Serla were heavily committed to investment in equipment at Sittingbourne to support the need for improved quality in an increasingly competitive marketplace.

In return, the management were charged with setting up a series of programmes to reduce costs, both fixed and variable over the next few years. Typical of these were the "Going for Broke" and "Commitment to Consistency" (CtC) projects.

But, firstly, in excess of £20m was earmarked for the Sittingbourne site and over little more than a two year period between 2000 and 2002, virtually every area of the Mill was to see some activity.

The first area to receive attention was stock preparation. Most visible was the bale handling system. Bales of pulp from around the world continued to be delivered into the Church Street entrance at the rear of the Mill but now they were de-stacked and transported to the hydrapulpers using fully automated de-wiring stations, metal detectors and conveyor systems. To support this, a new hydrapulper was built and extra refining capacity introduced.

Manual reel handling had been a source of damage over the years. To eliminate this, a Trancel transport system was laid around the Jubilee Street area to take reels from the winders to the shrinkwrap machine, the reels travelling on a complex system of conveyors and turntables.

All four coating heads on both coaters were fitted with fully computerised control – ProCoat. Although not new to the paper industry, this was a major step for improved quality at Sittingbourne. By using a bank of intelligent "actuators" across the width of the paper, the coat weights could be controlled to within a few microns to give a very even coatweight.

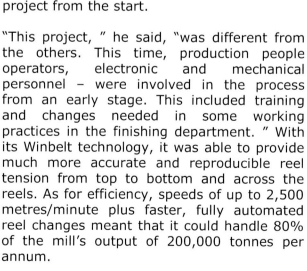

Perhaps the most significant investment was 41 reeler, at nearly £4m the largest single item. 41 reeler brought both efficiency and improved quality to the Mill.

Mark O'Gallagher was involved with the project from the start.

"This project, " he said, "was different from the others. This time, production people operators, electronic and mechanical personnel – were involved in the process from an early stage. This included training and changes needed in some working practices in the finishing department. " With its Winbelt technology, it was able to provide much more accurate and reproducible reel tension from top to bottom and across the reels. As for efficiency, speeds of up to 2,500 metres/minute plus faster, fully automated reel changes meant that it could handle 80% of the mill's output of 200,000 tonnes per annum.

Later, with a state-of-the-art reel inspection system fitted, 41 reeler provided one of the most important benefits to the improved quality of the Nimrod brand in the 1990's and into the 2000's.

On the calenders, an online profile control system known as Calcoil was added. By adjusting minute temperature increments across the reel, properties such as gloss and caliper could be monitored to very fine tolerances. This provided a more consistent profile across the full width of the reel.

Alistair Smith, Project Director responsible for the investment programme said, "All the investments made during this six month period are intended to improve the consistency of the product. Having listened to our customers, this is the one property of Nimrod that needed to be improved. Since the new equipment was installed, the benefits have been very obvious. "

Away from the Sittingbourne site, a vast pallet warehouse was constructed at Kemsley. At 120,000 square feet, and with racking over 70 feet high, the warehouse was designed to hold nearly 26,000 pallets from both the Kemsley site and Sittingbourne.

Whilst all this was going on, Metsa Serla had embarked on a programme of acquisition and divestment to realign the business more towards the core markets of fine paper and board manufacture. Gone were the sawn goods and building division, corrugated packaging and tissue interests. Into the family came Biberist Paper Mill in Switzerland, Modo Paper and Zanders. A major re-branding exercise took place and the name m-real was born.

m·real

With these investments in place, the Mill embarked on a series of initiatives designed to support the investments and to build on the improvements in quality that had already been achieved. The first, known as "Going For Broke", concentrated on minimising the quantity of "broke" (or paper waste) produced throughout the mill but not at the expense of quality. This resulted in record material efficiency.

Then, in 2002, Sittingbourne set out its business goals for the future in its "Business Vision for 2005". Encapsulated in this Vision was the Commitment to Consistency (CtC) business change programme. Sittingbourne committed itself to delivering consistent and reliable products and services and said it would differentiate itself by becoming the leading service provider to the UK's coated customers.

Business Vision for Sittingbourne 2005

We will deliver consistent and reliable product and service to the UK market We will always fulfil our commitments.

Sittingbourne will differentiate itself by becoming the leading service provider to the UK coated customer.

While retaining our current business, we will double our market share in coated sheets by 2005.

We will develop the Sittingbourne team to deliver consistency and be prepared to meet the future market needs and demands.

"Consistency is important, " said Nick Carter, Mill Manager, "because one of the things we have suffered from in the past is inconsistent quality. And we believe that focusing on service is one thing that is potentially unique to Sittingbourne because we are so close to the main UK markets."

Teamwork and the involvement of staff throughout the mill were integral to the strategy, says Carter. "We recognised that for this to be successful we had to change the whole culture of the organisation. It would do no good having a small group of people working on this." Shop floor input proved a vitally important means of identifying ways to improve the performance of the mill.

The CtC logo, designed by employee Alex Delamain, shows the bringing together of diverse information into one consistent line.

One of the early phases of the project was, therefore, to set up teams from a mix of disciplines to "brainstorm" ideas. Of more than 1000 that came out of this process – some simply, many more complex – in excess of 110 were adopted and implemented. By 2005, both paper machines were regularly delivering record time efficiency figures; customer complaint levels were reduced to a new – and stable – low level; service issues were greatly reduced.

Three of the winners of the 2004 Project Paint Competition hanging in the Finishing area. Each is 10 x 6 metres in size.

There was also a major cultural change in Sittingbourne Mill's external relations, with the mill taking an increasingly active role in the local community. One of the most visible aspects of this was the enormous reproductions of paintings by local school children who took part in an environmental competition called Project Paint. These hung from 2004 in the Finishing area and were an interesting talking point for visitors to the mill. The mill actively sponsored the local historical group and staff were encouraged to get involved in regular fund raising activities for the mill's lead charity, Demelza House. "Local initiatives are part of a more open culture, "said Nick Carter. "Four or five years ago we would never have dreamt of advertising Sittingbourne in that sense."

The Mayoral Visit

Wednesday 26th July 2006 was another very special day for local community relations when Sittingbourne Mill paid host to a group of local dignitaries and the press.

After a welcome from Nick Carter, Mill Manager, the guests were shown a presentation describing Sittingbourne Mill's excellent environmental credentials and products. There followed an extensive mill tour, with Nick Carter accompanying the Mayor and Mayoress. The guests were treated to a fascinating insight into the art of papermaking. For the majority of our guests, this was the first time they had had the opportunity to see round the mill.

In conjunction with our friends at the Historical Research Group of Sittingbourne, who had helped facilitate the day, it was also an opportunity to officially launch the wonderful Bowater Archive that REXAM supplied to us in 2005 making Mreal and the HRGS joint custodians. This archive is a treasure trove which includes such things as hand-made paper made on the site in the 1700's, with early photographs and documents charting our history.

All our guests thoroughly enjoyed the day at Sittingbourne Mill, leaving with an enhanced understanding of our process. Much feedback was received which included words such as 'fantastic' and hidden gem'.

Pictured right: (front row – left to right) Darryl Hardy, Alex Delamain, Gary Wood, (back row) Alan Amos – HRGS, Helen Morris – Print Week Magazine, Mayoress of Swale Mrs Ann Morris, Mayor of Swale Councillor John Morris, Nick Carter, Christine Rayner, - East Kent Gazette, Kevan Atkins – Sittingbourne Library, Bill Croydon CBE – HRGS President, Clare Cook – M-real External Communications UK, Lyn Newton – Swale Borough Council, Deborah Saunders & Lynn Finn – Kent County Council, Michael H. Peters.

With CtC established as "A way of life", the mill continued to provide quality and consistency to its customers. During the later years, the marketplace was becoming increasingly aware of its environmental responsibilities, driven by both Government and public awareness. The pulp and paper industry became under particular scrutiny because of its reliance on forest products. Two issues were at the forefront – forestry certification and recycling.

Era Silk

With pressure for recycling in the UK increasing, Sittingbourne was now in a unique position to benefit from the existence of the Recycled Fibre Plant at Kemsley. Where EVOLVE Coated had failed in 1997, the experiences gained in the intervening years enabled Sittingbourne to develop a new recycled product for the 21st century – Era Silk. The philosophy behind Era Silk was simple – to provide a product with unparalleled environmental credentials for the UK market. Existing "environmental" products in the UK were lacking the local benefits that Era Silk could offer. The waste paper for recycling was collected and processed locally; the paper was made locally and it was distributed locally. Within its mixture of 50% recycled pulp and 50% virgin pulp, Era Silk used only virgin pulp from certified sources.

Examples of corporate communication documents printed using Era Silk.

All these unique benefits were considered ideal for large corporate organisations who were looking to improve their own environmental responsibility. Era Silk was the breakthrough they were seeking – high quality combined with environmental credentials unparalleled for a coated recycled paper.

Era Silk was launched in 2006 and made an immediate impact. Sales through two leading merchants improved month on

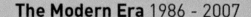
month and many blue chip companies were using the product for their Corporate Communications. These included Marks & Spencer, Standard Life, HSBC and Wolseley plc plus many Government departments. Sales continued to increase right up until the closure of the mill.

Its sister product, Era Print, an uncoated option also containing 50% recycled pulp, was about to be launched and had already generated considerable interest.

Unfortunately after many years of rumour, the notice of closure came in October 2006 and the mill was shut on the 31st January 2007. The last reel of paper off PM15 was at 09:32 on the 23rd January, PM16 10:37 on the 28th January and the last set reel off Reeler 41 at 22:08 also on the 28th January 2007. The last reels off the machines saw the end of papermaking at the site after more than 300 years of history.

The final reel of base paper from PM15 – 09.32 on 23rd January 2007.

The End

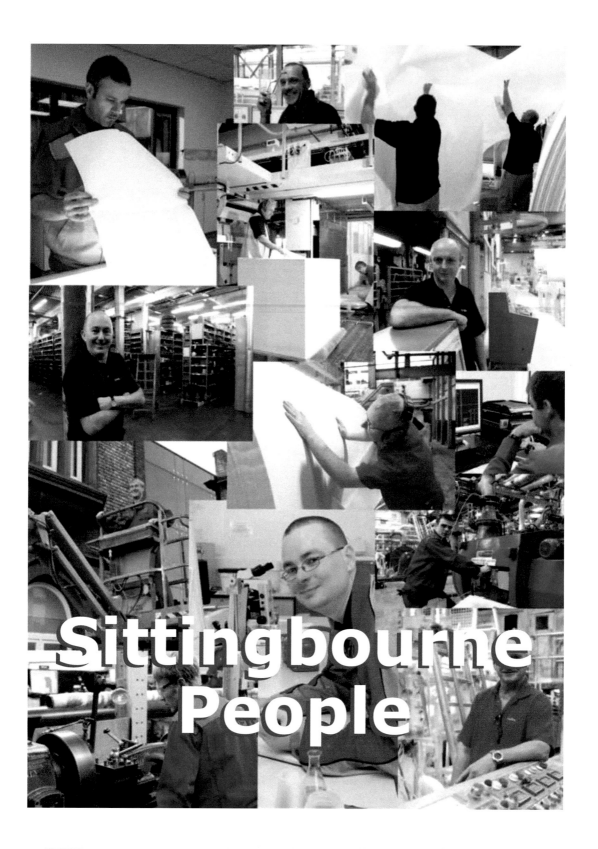

Sittingbourne People

A paper mill is as much about people as machines, if not more so, and Sittingbourne was no exception. Over the years many thousands of people have passed through the mill, often several generations of the same family.

The memories and recollections of just a few of these people are published over the next few pages. Also included are pictures taken just prior to the closure of the mill in January 2007 of three of the Shifts (Shifts A and C were not available), the Production and Technical Departments and the Engineers.

One common thread through these memories is that of the friendships that were formed through working at the mill. Arguably, some of this may be attributed to the fundamental roots that were laid down in the early 1900's by Frank Lloyd who adopted a very benevolent attitude towards his workforce.

"I earned nine shillings a week for a seventy eight hour week. We got no holidays but, after we had been there for a year, were given a free railway ticket for a day at Margate."

The Killin family l. to r. Andy, Bert, Joe and Tom.

The Killin Family

One of the most remarkable families ever associated with the mill was the Killin family. At one time father and four sons worked there.

"Old Tom" Killin – as the father was known – started at Sittingbourne in 1894. His sons all began there as reeler boys. In an article in Bowater World in April 1961, Tom, then seventy six, said proudly, "the Killin family has always been in paper making. My grandfather and his father before him were paper makers in Scotland.

Sittingbourne People

"I started at Sittingbourne when I was just thirteen," he continued. "I earned nine shillings a week for a seventy eight hour week. We got no holidays but, after we had been there for a year, were given a free railway ticket for a day at Margate. "

"I would start work at six o'clock on Friday evening and work round to six o'clock in the morning. Then I just had time to dash home for a quick wash and catch the 7.30 train to Margate. "

One of his most vivid memories is of the day in 1900 when the mill was almost destroyed by fire. Tom was working there when the fire broke out.

"I remember clearly standing there by the machine, open mouthed, watching the flames catch the paper," he said, "It was a terrible blaze." During the fire-fighting, an important priority, apparently, was the supply of beer for the thirsty firemen. A nearby pub was opened and ten gallon casks of beer were quickly ordered.

Bill Hilliard

Recorded in Bowater World of April 1961 are the memories of Bill Hilliard.

Bill began work at Sittingbourne in 1889 as a reeler boy. "When I started, " he said, "I earned five shillings. In those days, the men on the night shifts would be paid at the end of the shift by the foreman of the beater-men; and to save the cashier getting up in the small hours of the morning, the money would be handed out in a pub near the mill. Inevitably, some of it would find its way over the counter!

"When I joined, the raw material used was esparto grass. There would be lots of weeds in the grass and boys were employed to sift them out. "Before they finished, the boys had to show a pile of weeds to prove they had done a hard day's work. They soon found a way round this one. On good days, they would carefully hoard a bunch of weeds for the time when they wanted to take it easy."

In those days motor cars and lorries had not been invented. All the coal was carried by horse from the wharf. Said Bill, "I can remember times when there would be a long line of carts stretching for about a mile down the road, like a gypsy funeral procession."

Tony Gregory

Tony originally joined the company back in 1955, thanks to his father using his influence, who at the time was Yard Foreman. Tony spent the next 3 years as Assistant Salle Porter in the old No.4 Salle and progressed on to become Salle Porter. In 1958 Tony left to join the RAF for 3 years regular service, as being young he wanted to be a Fighter Pilot, but instead finished up behind the officers mess bar.

He left the RAF and by 1962 had returned to the mill, spending the next 2 years at the Wharf working on the corrugator machine until it was sold. He was then transferred back to the Conversion Department as a Cutter Assistant until 1972, and then took the role as Deputy Shift Foreman until 1975 when he was promoted to full Shift Foreman, a post he held until 1986. He was then given a temporary day work position due to day staff sickness and also worked on small projects within the Conversion Department.

When both the Conversion Manager and Day Superintendent retired in the late 80's and a new Conversion Manager took over, he was again put on day work for the purpose of increasing the throughput of the cutters. After about a year he was promoted to Conversion Superintendent and also a short spell as Deputy Conversion Manager, continuing as Superintendent until Tony took early retirement in 2000.

But Tony was soon back under contract to carry out various duties including training and qualifying Operators on Cutters, Ream Packer, Baler, and Core Stripper at New Thames. His time was spent updating and writing SOP's (Safe Operating Procedures) for Sittingbourne and New Thames Conversion, as well as helping to increase throughput on the Cutters.

Tony says that he made lots of friends and enjoyed working with everyone over the years and misses that friendship.

Don Rouse
Early memories of Sittingbourne Mill

Don joined Sittingbourne mill in 1936 when the company was still known as Edward Lloyd, at the age of 16 following in the footsteps of grandfather, father and two elder brothers who had all worked at the mill. Don still recalls his mother saying to him, "At six o'clock tonight I want you to go and see Mr Brightman", he was the Chief Papermaker, the equivalent of a Mill Manager today.

He lived in a big house in the Tunstall area. I remember arriving at the house and a maid showed me into Mr Brightman's study, "Sit yourself down boy, now you are Rouse's boy aren't you. Your father was a good man, a good employee, a very good man of the company and if we employ you I want you to be the same", "Yes sir! ", "You start at the mill on Monday and I want you to learn as much as you can because in a year or so we have other plans".

In 1936 there were over 1000 people at the mill including 200 women working in the Salle. 17 machines were in operation, which included four machines running in the Old Mill but No. 1 and No. 3 machines stopped shortly after. No. 4 made wood pulp reeled up wet for a packaging plant at Northfleet. In the main mill Machine No's 14, 15, 16 & 17 manufactured newsprint.

Roll coating was beginning to be used with No.11 being the first to make base for coating followed by No.12. The smaller machines, No's 5, 6, 7, 8 & 9 were all scrapped just before WW2 and were sent to Germany; a year later they probably came back again as bombs!.

A few months after he joined, the mill was acquired by Bowater's and it was then known as Bowater Lloyd. The general feeling was this was a good thing as there had been very little investment in recent years.

When I started we did not have any QC. The Machineman at the wet end simply had a quadrant and a micrometer. If the paper was within 5% of the weight and 2% of the thickness it was sold. Don established the Main Lab which was situated in the main office building to the left of the main entrance doors. The lab equipment included an Ingersoll Glarimeter for gloss and a Becks smoothness tester. All samples had to be brought across from the mill but if it was a damp day this affected the samples.

Don's elder brother worked on the papermaking side as a dryerman/1st assistant and due to an accident was excused from any Army service. In those days there were no rope feeds and all the machine calender rolls were hand fed. When the paper came through from the last cylinder it had to be thrown into the calender rolls. There was a plank he would sit on with the rolls thundering away in front of him, when the dry end tail came through he would get hold of it and throw it into the first nip. This would make his feet automatically come up and one occasion his toes went into the rolls. After the war the mill had its own first aid unit and after a clear out of the ambulance room he remembers 'Tiny Allan' saying " I have something you might be interested in", it turned out to be a glass jar containing three solid grisly bits where were my brother's toes!.

"With WW2 I went to recruitment and going in the Army was the only choice I had. I was sent to Normandy and all our shells came in metal cases with a cardboard tube protecting the shells. Picking out my shells there was a stamp "BL" – Bowater Lloyd, I said to myself, 'God – I wish I was back there!' "

Peter Graham

I started work in No1 Salle which was a packing Salle working as a Porter. I did that job for just a week as I was asked if I would like to do export packing. For the 1980 Moscow Olympics I can remember packing 1500 pallets of paper for the Olympic programmes and this resulted in a lot of overtime to ensure the order left on time.

The Mill has been a major part of my life, whilst at the mill I even met my wife Lisa in 1977 who worked in the Salle hand sorting paper, we have been happily married for 25 years this year. For ten years I was pallet loading and then for

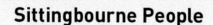

Sittingbourne People

three years I was a lubrication technician, but most recently for the past five years have been Store man at Sittingbourne Mill. One of the main things I will miss will be the camaraderie with all my colleagues and all the fun times on days and on shift.

Brenda Gasson

I started in the mill at the age of 15 in 1963 and was one of over 300 women working in the Salle. I was not used to being amongst so many women!! It was my uncle that got me the job and many other family members had worked there as well. In the Salle in those early days it was a very strict regime. There was no talking and you had to put your hand up if you wanted to go to the toilet.

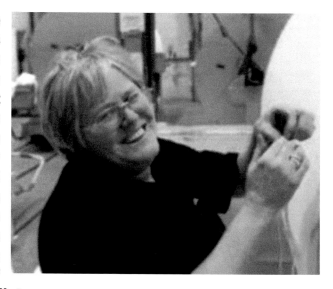

The older women played tricks on the Salle boys. Short skirts and high heels were the norm and there were no safety shoes or ear plugs! The lift kept breaking down and we were never allowed to go anywhere near the machines. Jean Wildish was the supervisor and
Rose Barker trained me.

I left in 1968 to raise my family but was back in 1997, from which time I worked in various parts of the mill. Starting in Conversion, I moved to Finishing then to work on No. 1 prewinder and No. 1 coater. The one thing that I shall miss when the mill shuts is the people I worked with – I have never known anything else and it was like a family.

Colin Stone

I started work at the mill in 1972. I was earning £11 per week at Tesco but the mill was willing to up this to £18! My first impression was that everything was so big. I first worked as a Service Operator in Jubilee Street and my job was to collect up all the broke and take it away in massive wooden trucks. There were no electric transporters in those days, it was all done by hand.

I remember that when I started the mill had its own fire fighters and ambulance and there was a nurse on duty 24 hours a day. And they were all dressed so immaculately! I also remember that there was one guy who spent his whole day at work cleaning the toilets.

All the reels had to be packed by hand, and it was an awful job, and worse in the winter as the lorries would go from Jubilee Street and when the doors went up you would get an icy blast, and be working with frozen hands. If there was no work in other departments they would send you there, this became known as the 'Knackers Yard'. There was a good atmosphere in the mill and we had some good fun. With all the different characters, it could be a bit boisterous and they were always up to tricks! I will miss all the people that I worked with.

Dick Craycraft

I started at the mill in 1959 at the age of 15 as a Mill Clerks Runner. I would go around the mill with notices etc and remember how amazed I was at seeing so many people with fingers missing.

This was mainly due to so much feeding up of the machines by hand, much different from today. At that time there were 8 paper machines, a straw plant and iron foundry in operation.

I had visited the mill on a school visit when I was 14 years old and remember the machineman on PM12 saying that I would be wasting my time coming to work here, I suppose 47 years on he was right.

I started in production when I was just over 16 years old on PM17 as a Press Boy.

Every Saturday night the machines would be washed out, and when they shut down lots of carpenters would appear as many areas of the machines were made of wood.

My best memory when I leave will be of all the blokes and all the fun, and if I had the opportunity I would do my 47 years all over again.

John Ives

I started work at SB Mill on PM14 stencilling and packing. My first impressions were the smell from the machine (the smell only papermakers would recognise) making heavy weight liner and how dark it was. I worked there for two weeks then moved on to PM16 as 'first boy'.

At that time PM17 was alongside. I was part of team that comprised the machine man, press boy, dryer man, spare dryer man and first boy and on top of this there was a reserve dryer man who worked across the two machines splicing ropes etc.

There was a very strong community spirit in those days backed up by many inter-shift sporting events such as football, cricket and ten pin bowling. The shift pattern was 7 days of nights, two days off, then 7 days of 2-10 then two off and 7 days of 6-2 two days off. The mill was shut for two weeks in the summer and a week at Christmas. One of the biggest achievements of Sittingbourne Mill has been to modernise communications between the unions and management to the benefit of both the individual and the company which has played a great part in modernising technology and working practices.

One lasting memory is the ability to approach any member of the mill management speaking openly and freely about almost any issue and be listened to. So much has been achieved over the mill's last seven years and this was appreciated by suppliers, visitors and customers alike.

Brian Williams

My first impression of Sittingbourne Mill? The smell!! As I came from the station there was a general smell around, and a strong smell of rotten eggs (hydrogen sulphide) coming from the local creek which contained a few years of effluent deposits!

When I joined in 1977, my first job was Coating Chemist and Nos. 14, 15, 16 and 17 machines were running. I remember the original PM15 Massey Roll Coater which gave us a lot of problems. I was more involved with the blade coater which was a much superior process and later worked as Coating Manager and Technical Manager.

One of the highlights over the years must be the installation of the new PM15. Malcolm Boorman and Barry Butler were the main drivers behind its purchase, with a little help from Monty August who was responsible for raising the £23m needed for the project. PM14 never stopped during the installation and I remember the huge temporary plastic roof that was erected to stop the rain getting in. With all the steam condensing under the cover, it often became very foggy. Once PM15 was commissioned, this was a tremendous morale booster to the mill.

Whilst on a trip to visit Measurex in Italy with Barry Butler, we saw a coater which had been mothballed and decided to buy it there and then. It was the sister machine to the one already in Sittingbourne both being made by Rice Barton in the mid 60's. A deal was struck and we purchased the extra coater so that the mill could start to produce the better quality double coated papers. This is what we now know as No. 1 coater but it has been rebuilt considerably since the early Italian model was bought.

I will miss the people. Equipment is just machinery but Sittingbourne has always been a nice place to work because of the people I have worked with.

Sittingbourne People

Technical & Production Departments

Brian Williams – Technical Manager, Karen Hills, David Bunyan, Alex Delamain, Steve Foster, Alex Ashton, Louise Harrison, Mark Hammond – Production Manager, Simon Pointer, Simon Tyler, Teemu Makkonen, Nick Carter – Mill Manager, Caron Brislee – Shift Manager (Days), Darryl Hardy, Mark O'Gallagher - Shift Manager (Days), Ian Taylor.

B Shift

Derick Norris, John Hutchinson, Norman Homewood, Tim Clark, Nigel Freeman, Russell Higgins, Dave Simler, Rob Minchin, Tony Eldridge, Jamie Cantelow, Paul Still, Martin Brazier, Rhys Edmunds, Paul Simmers, Andy Rea, Jez Dawson, Glenn Miles, James McGee, Tony Stelfox, Graham King, Ed Rapley, Bob Harrison, Clive Ratcliff, Barrie Edwards, Glen Hills, Robin Tinker, Dave Hurn, Paul Bennett, Greg Stone – Shift Manager, John Crawford, Martin Wells, James McGee, Paul Downs.

D Shift

Gerry Peckham, Gary Clements, Lee Kennett, Mark Reed, Simon Rooney, Andy Coomber, Kevin Walder, Michael Baker, Kevin Belsom, Colin Stone – Shift Manager, Joe Mannouch, Dave Rose, Nigel Woodfine, Tony McElhone, Paul Warner, Ian Trower, Jamie King, Percy Bootes, Mark Allen, Alan Tumber, Andy Danton, John Ives, Rob Crutchley, Richard Kennett, Michael Humphreys, Nick Brooker, Adam Faram, Vaughan Gilks

E Shift

Richard Gisby, John Holtum, Russell Townsley, Andy Wakeling, Tom Tucker, Tony Baker, Peter Tucker, Bob Cope, Richard Young, Bob Bourne, John Sandy, Arthur Stokes, Lee Crosswell, Lawrence Kent, Keith Humphrey, Steve Wellard, Michael Parady, Damon Mitchell, Mark Slingsby, Bill Lockwood, Alan Richmond, Sean Collins, Paul Willett, Kevin Aldworth, Bill Stone, Mark Pamplin, Andrew Kemp, Peter Thompson, Malcolm Beaney, Gary Jennings, Mark Fenn – A shift, Chris Butcher – Shift Manager

Engineering Department

Dave Kelly, Mick Jeffrey, Dave Eede, Jim Logan, Paul Onslow, Gary Warner, Dick Wild, Tim Merner, Mark Cunningham, Peter Delman, Tony Strike, Andy Searle, Ross Pilcher, Martin Gray, John Hawkins, Keith Mummery, Paul Price, Ray Iles, Steve Bootes, Elaine Dighton, Mike Crocker, Norman Foord, Mark Harris, Terry Salt, Richard Woolston, Mick Clemons, Dave Mills, Steve Hannon, Malcolm Mesher, Jamie Pankhurst, Paul Woolley, Keith Weatherley, Mark Lovett, Bruce Groom, Steve Bartlett, Alec Provan, John Eede, Steve Lee, Mark Wootten, Paul Byrne, Ian Upton, Tony Devine, Adam Dobner, Simon Locks

View from the water tower: Staff clocking off at shift change

Postface

The Sittingbourne Paper Mill was demolished between 2010 and 2012 and a new supermarket built on the eastern part of the site. Houses have been built on the western part of the site and one of the new streets has been named Bowater Close.

In 2021, papermaking continues at the Kemsley Mill site.

Sittingbourne Heritage Museum

Sittingbourne has had a museum since 1999. It is a registered charity, and is funded by its membership. Our aims are:

> *The advancement of the education of the public in the history of Sittingbourne and Milton Regis and the surrounding areas by the provision of a local heritage centre.*

Currently located at 67 East Street, the museum houses many objects from Sittingbourne and the surrounding villages which have been donated or loaned by local residents and other museums.

Apart from caring for our collection, behind the scenes, researchers are peering into the town's past, and then producing highly respected books or videos on various topics related to the history of our area.

Please help support the Museum by becoming a member. Members receive a regular newsletter and a quarterly copy of our Journal with essays on aspects of local history for Sittingbourne and the surrounding area.

www.sittingbourne-museum.co.uk